the Art of
LEADERSHIP

LEADING
EARLY CHILDHOOD ORGANIZATIONS

Exchange Press

7700 A Street

Lincoln, Nebraska 68510

(800) 221-2864 • ExchangePress.com

Leading Early Childhood Organizations

The Art of Leadership series replaces the popular Exchange Press textbook, *The Art of Leadership: Managing Early Childhood Organizations*. The entire series demonstrates the great complexity of an early childhood leader's job. Each volume expresses the importance of one aspect of this role. Each leader will need to prioritize all these roles based on many factors, including the skills that reside within the members of his team.

These articles were originally published in *Exchange* magazine.
Every attempt has been made to update information on authors and other contributors to these articles. We apologize for any biographical information that is not current.
Exchange is a bimonthly management magazine for directors, owners, and teachers of early childhood programs. For more information about *Exchange* and other Exchange Press publications for directors and teachers, contact:

Exchange Press
7700 A Street
Lincoln, Nebraska 68510
(800) 221-2864 • ExchangePress.com

ISBN 978-0-942702-58-3

Printed in the United States
© Dimensions Educational Research Foundation, 2019

Cover Design: Scott Bilstad

the Art of
LEADERSHIP
LEADING
EARLY CHILDHOOD ORGANIZATIONS

Introduction

What Has 14 Hands? *by Bonnie Neugebauer and Roger Neugebauer* 5

Chapter 1: Being a Leader

Being a Boss *by Roger Neugebauer* 8

Heart-centered Leadership *by Nancy Rosenow* 17

Leadership Matters: Creating Anti-bias Change in
Early Childhood Programs *by Louise Derman-Sparks, John Nimmo, and Debbie LeeKeenan* 21

Effective Leadership Behaviors for Child Care Administrators *by Rachel Robertson* 26

The Role of Knowledge in Leadership *by Maurice Sykes* 30

Spreading the Wealth: Leadership at All Levels *by Debra R. Sullivan* 34

So You're a Director — What Else Can Go Wrong? *by Roger Neugebauer* 38

The Art of Leadership: What We've Learned in 38 Years
by Bonnie Neugebauer and Roger Neugebauer 41

Chapter 2: Supervising Staff

12 Reasons People Love to Work for You *by Roger Neugebauer* 46

Who Made Me Boss? *by Gigi Schweikert* 51

Self-Motivation: Motivation at Its Best *by Roger Neugebauer* 54

What Do Teachers Need Most from Their Directors? *by Margie Carter* 60

The Paradoxes of Leadership *by Bonnie Neugebauer and Roger Neugebauer* 65

You Say Staff Deserve Respect? Energize Your Words with Action! *by Karen Stephens* 69

Becoming an Authentic Communicator *by Johnna Darragh Ernst* 73

Building and Rebuilding Your Credibility *by Roger Neugebauer* 77

If Your Boss is the Problem, What Choices Do You Have? *by Holly Elissa Bruno* 81

Chapter 3: Managing the Organization

ECE and Business Savvy — A Happy Marriage *by Cecelia Doyle* 92

Are You Running a Center or Building an Organization?
by Joan Dunn Antonsen, Jan Silverman, and Pauline Work 95

Searching for Innovators: An Interview with Louise Stoney *by Margie Carter* 101

New Ways of Managing: Alternative Approaches to Leading
Early Childhood Organizations *by Roger Neugebauer* 107

Becoming Community Centric *by Lisa Ann Haeseler* 110

Growing a Multi-site Organization: Build Systems of Credibility and
Empower Others to Execute Them *by Chad Dunkley* 114

Nine Questions for the Dedicated Board Member *by Roger Neugebauer* 117

Enjoying the Good Lice: Managing Crises *by Pauline Davey Zeece* 119

Considering Expansion? Lessons Learned Along the Way *by Henry Wilde* 123

Out of the Box Ideas on Center Evaluation by *Roger Neugebauer* 128

Do You Have a Healthy Organization? *by Roger Neugebauer* 132

What Has 14 Hands?

by Bonnie Neugebauer and Roger Neugebauer

In a recent commercial a young promising techie announces that he was just hired by General Electric. The reaction of his family and friends is disappointment — they perceive that with this career choice his promising career in high tech has just gone off the rails.

A center director once related a similar story. She was at a party when someone asked her what she did. When she announced she was an early childhood director, the person responded, "Well that's not rocket science, is it?"

From the outside it may indeed appear that a director's job is easy — all you have to do is keep a bunch of kids occupied all day and then collect fees from thankful parents. Little do they know that leading an early childhood center really is rocket science!

In 1978, when we launched *Exchange Magazine*, we sent out a flyer which asked...

As our flyer implied, an effective early childhood director must be proficient in a wide range of roles. They must be...

- **Leaders** — directing the efforts of all the players involved in the organization to achieve its goals

- **Financial managers** — developing and monitoring the implementation of the budget, managing receivables and payables, dealing with cash flow crises

What Has 14 Hands?

Two for slashing budgets,

Two for writing proposals,

Two for making fluffernutters,

Two for repairing Big Wheels,

Two for changing diapers,

And four for fending off bureaucrats.

- **Customer service specialists** — welcoming, supporting, and communicating with a diverse mix of parents

- **Professional development specialists** — recruiting great staff, training them, appraising their performance and promoting teamwork.

- **Marketing and advocacy experts** — promoting enrollment, building your center's reputation, and advocating for policies that protect and support children and families.

- **Curriculum planners** — understanding child development, crafting a curriculum, designing spaces, and evaluating the program.

This entire *Art of Leadership* series is designed to address the wide range of responsibilities that come with the job of early childhood director. It draws upon the wisdom of the leading experts in early childhood education. And, most importantly, it respects the value of the role early childhood leaders play in supporting the children, families, and communities they serve, as well as the individuals they employ and the profession they belong to.

Bonnie Neugebauer

Bonnie Neugebauer is Editor of *Exchange Magazine* and a co-founder of the World Forum Foundation.

Roger Neugebauer

Roger Neugebauer is publisher of *Exchange Magazine* and a co-founder of the World Forum Foundation.

the *Art of*
LEADERSHIP
LEADING
EARLY CHILDHOOD ORGANIZATIONS

1 CHAPTER 1
Being a Leader

Being a Boss *by Roger Neugebauer* 8

Heart-centered Leadership *by Nancy Rosenow* 17

Leadership Matters: Creating Anti-bias Change in
Early Childhood Programs *by Louise Derman-Sparks, John Nimmo, and Debbie LeeKeenan* 21

Effective Leadership Behaviors for Child Care Administrators *by Rachel Robertson* 26

The Role of Knowledge in Leadership *by Maurice Sykes* 30

Spreading the Wealth: Leadership at All Levels *by Debra R. Sullivan* 34

So You're a Director — What Else Can Go Wrong? *by Roger Neugebauer* 38

The Art of Leadership: What We've Learned in 38 Years
by Bonnie Neugebauer and Roger Neugebauer 41

Being a Boss

by Roger Neugebauer

The effective boss is one who possesses a high concern for influencing people toward the benefit of the organization.

Don't try to use your position to make people love you, and don't expect that people will obey you because they love you.

A People-Oriented Boss, who cares mainly about stimulating high-performance by staff members, provides objective feedback to them, knowing this will help them improve their performance.

Child care directors come in all shapes, sizes, and styles. One thing you all have in common is a genuine concern for people. As you well know, sometimes this concern for people can get in the way of your being effective as a director. At times you would rather be a friend to the staff members than their boss. You want very much for all staff members to like you and to follow your lead as director because they like you, not because they fear you.

Unfortunately, it can't always work out this way. You find that you are forced to make some decisions that won't please everyone or, on occasion, anyone. You find that no matter how friendly you try to be, staff members are often cautious and somewhat distant in their relations with you, even though they may be open and easy going in their relations with each other. Sometimes it seems like the harder you try to please everyone, the more they resent it.

What you are experiencing is 'status anxiety.' This is that seemingly inevitable tension — that invisible wall — that arises between director and staff. While this anxiety is a feeling that nearly all directors experience at some point in their careers, it is also a feeling that can be successfully dealt with.

This article describes a number of approaches that are guaranteed to fail, as well as many that are likely to succeed, in relieving status anxiety. Before reviewing these suggestions, you might want to take a few minutes to assess how well you are succeeding in balancing your desire to be a friend and your need to be a boss. The more of the following questions you can answer with "yes," the better. Then try out some of the suggestions that follow, and check yourself out in six months to see if you are making progress.

How Do You Rate as a Boss?

1. When you enter a room of staff members, does conversation continue?

2. Are staff meetings chaired by you lively and honest?

3. Is staff turnover, especially for key people in your center, very low?

4. Do staff members regularly come to you for advice?

5. Do staff members freely voice conflicting opinions on center issues?

6. When a decision is made, do staff members faithfully carry it out?

7. Although gossip seldom reaches you, do you always hear about center problems before they become crises?

8. When you delegate a task to a staff member, do you stop worrying about it?

9. Do staff members freely give you feedback on your performance?

10. When you encounter staff members unexpectedly outside the center, do they appear to be genuinely pleased to see you?

How Not to be a Boss

The Benevolent Boss

Sometimes one's need to be loved is so strong that all other demands take a back seat. The director giving in to this need, trying the Benevolent Boss approach, seeks to make everyone on staff love her. She strives to be perceived as everyone's buddy, as just one of the gang.

The Benevolent Boss uses her position and personality to try to please everyone. She is overflowing in praise and sparing with criticism. She seeks to win staff members over with favors — going out of her way to provide supplies teachers ask for; bending the rules for individuals experiencing personal problems; overlooking deficiencies in job performance; loaning her books, her car, her money. The personal lives of staff members become a major concern of hers. To keep everyone happy, this amiable administrator never overlooks an opportunity to throw a party.

The Disappearing Boss

One temptation for a director who feels uncomfortable with the trappings of power is to play down his authority and play up his likeability. This is an exercise in 'status stripping' — whereby the director tries to disregard all the symbols of status and authority (Zaleznik).

The Disappearing Boss eschews all appearances of pretension and privilege. He uses the cheapest desk available, and his chair is the oldest (and preferably the most uncomfortable) in the center. A spartan motif prevails throughout his office — if he has an office at all (some uneasy executives locate themselves in some dimly lit corner or in a breezy entryway). In dress, he is as nondescript as possible — he's an annual fixture on *Exchange*'s "Worst Dressed Directors" list.

In his behavior, the Disappearing Boss likewise de-emphasizes his power. He answers his own phone and gets his own coffee. In staff meetings, he avoids sitting at the head of the table. He doesn't issue orders, he makes requests. When there is controversy about an issue, he avoids making a decision altogether, hoping the problem will go away.

The Workaholic Wonder

Another approach to ameliorating the effects of being the boss is for the director to work twice as hard as anybody else. The Workaholic Wonder convinces herself that staff members will be less likely to resent her authority if she earns their respect through hard work. She comes in before anyone else, is the last to leave every day, and lets it be known that she comes in on weekends. Not only does she refuse to delegate any of her tasks, but she insists on taking over the grubbiest of the teachers' jobs, such as picking up at the end of the day and cleaning the bathrooms.

These three approaches may do wonders for assuaging the director's sense of guilt over her special status, but they are shortsighted attempts to deny or obscure reality. Sooner or later they are bound to backfire. When the Benevolent Boss is forced to make an unpopular decision, Santa Claus will be exposed as just another boss, and her efforts to win popularity will be viewed as pure phoniness.

On the other hand, the Disappearing Boss and the Workaholic Wonder may be so successful at downplaying their status and authority that when the time comes to make a hard decision everyone will question their right to do so (Prentice). Rather than increasing the director's respect among staff members, these last two approaches are more likely to convince them that their boss is not operating with a full deck.

Another potential ill effect of these approaches is that attempts to avoid making unpopular decisions will do more to undermine staff morale than will the decisions themselves. If the director bends the rules for certain individuals, or overlooks their poor performance, other staff members are likely to become upset at this unfair or inequitable treatment.

Directors who continually avoid making hard decisions are likely to stimulate apprehension among staff members. Studies by David C. McClellan tend to support these conclusions. He found that managers who place their need to be liked above all other considerations tend to have subordinates who feel that they have very little personal responsibility, that organizational procedures are not clear, and that they have little pride in their work group. Their employees feel "... weak, irresponsible, and without a sense of what might happen next, of where they stand in relation to their manager, or even of what they ought to be doing" (McClellan).

The R2D2 Boss

An entirely different approach to resolving status anxiety is to try to perform like a robot — to take all feelings out of the process of managing. The R2D2 Boss is resigned to the conclusion that it is not possible for a boss to gain the friendship of his staff members. He therefore strives to perform his job in a very efficient, businesslike manner.

R2D2 focuses his attention on the goals of the center, and views the staff as a tool for accomplishing them. He makes specific assignments to all staff members and closely monitors their performance. Violations of rules and deficiencies in performance are dealt with quickly, fairly, and predictably. Time is viewed as a precious commodity not to be squandered on socializing and chit chat.

The Tyrannical Boss

Finally we have the boss who has completely thrown in the towel on human relations. Believing that staff members view all friendliness as a sign of weakness, the Tyrant seeks to rule with an iron hand. Staff members will be made to obey her not because they like her but because they fear her. Rules and assignments are spelled out in great detail and posted everywhere. Failure to comply with these requirements are dealt with swiftly and harshly.

It should come as no surprise that these last two impersonal approaches to being a boss are doomed to failure as well. These directors are clearly not inhibited by concerns about whether subordinates will like them, nor are their subordinates uncertain about what is expected of them. However, they make staff members feel like cogs in the machinery or slaves in the galley.

In studies of more than 5,000 organizations by Rensis Likert, it was found that totally 'production-oriented' managers were inaccessible, autocratic, and punitive. They were not good delegators. Their units were plagued with low morale and low productivity (Rogers).

How to Be a People-oriented Boss

The Benevolent Boss, the Disappearing Boss, and the Workaholic Wonder described above demonstrate (in overstated terms, of course) that a boss preoccupied with his need to be liked cannot succeed. On the other hand, R2D2 and the Tyrant make clear that a preoccupation with 'production' is not a healthy response to status anxiety either. So where does the answer lie? According to David C. McClellan, the effective boss is one who possesses a high concern for influencing people toward the benefit of the organization. This concern ought to be greater than her need to be liked by people, as well as her concern for production (McClellan). She is a 'people-oriented' boss. Her prime objective is to motivate members of her staff to work to their full potential to achieve the goals of the organization.

There is no set formula for becoming a People-Oriented Boss. Your management style will be influenced by the size and structure of the center you manage, as well as by your own personality and previous experiences with authority. However, a variety of studies have found that successful people-oriented bosses do have in common the ten characteristics described below.

#1. Be Realistic

There is no denying that your being a boss does affect your relationship with your subordinates. There is a maxim in the study of human behavior that describes this situation: "love flees authority." Where one individual has the capacity to control and affect the actions of another, the feeling governing this relationship tends to be one of distance and (hopefully) respect, but not one ultimately of warmth and friendliness (Zaleznik).

This does not mean that directors must resign themselves to a total lack of friendliness. In fact, if a boss cannot get along comfortably with subordinates, he will never be able to do his job well or enjoy it (Caplow). From having visited hundreds of child care centers across the country, this author has observed that many of the most effective directors do have warm relationships with their staff members. However, underlying even these relationships is a noticeable constraint. The role of the boss, even in a small, non-bureaucratic human service organization, brings with it some invisible barriers that can be largely overcome, but never totally erased.

Don't frustrate yourself with unrealistic expectations. Don't feel like you are a failure if staff members don't all love you. Above all, don't try to use your position to make people love you, and don't expect that people will obey you because they love you.

#2. Be Yourself

One way to relieve status anxiety is to establish a firm sense of identity — to know who you are and who you are not, to know what you are capable of and what you are not. Successful leaders exhibit all types of personalities. They are shy, gregarious, laid back, hyperactive, jocular, and humorless. There is no need to try to be someone you are not, to try to change your behavior based on what you think others want you to be.

By establishing a firm sense of identity, by being oneself, a director avoids what Abraham Zaleznik describes as "being buffeted around the sea of opinions he must live within." This sense of identity permits a freedom of action and thinking that is so necessary for effective leadership (Zaleznik).

#3. Be Consistent

Closely related to the need to be yourself is the necessity of maintaining a constancy in how you present yourself to others. Frequent, unpredictable changes in your behavior are confusing to your staff members. They are entitled to a sense of security that comes from a feeling of reasonable continuity in the responses of their boss (Zaleznik).

Staff members function optimally when they receive consistent signals from their boss in terms of performance standards, personnel policies, work assignments, and program emphases. For example, if a director is continually announcing new program emphases — one month proclaiming 'self image' the center's top priority and the next declaring 'reading readiness' the number one concern — staff members will become reluctant to invest too much effort or personal interest in any one project for fear it will be wasted.

Consistency in the administration of rewards and punishments is especially important. Employees need to know what efforts on their part will result in known rewards and what acts on their part will lead to known consequences. To be perceived as 'being fair' in this regard, a director must adhere to certain ground rules. Staff members should be informed clearly and in advance about their exact work assignments and performance standards. Likewise, center rules, and the penalties resulting from their infraction, should be made clear at the outset. The director then must be firm and consistent in administering rewards and punishments based on these known expectations (Hackman).

Failure to make expectations clear at the outset will cause uncertainty and frustration. Failure to enforce them consistently will result in hostility and loss of credibility and respect for the director.

#4. Be a Goal Setter

A key task for any boss is to focus the attention and efforts of staff members on the goals of the organization. The organization can be most successful if all staff members are channeling their efforts in the same direction. Likewise, staff members can be most effective if it is clear where they should be directing their efforts.

One hoped for outcome of focusing attention on organizational goals is the building of loyalty of staff members to the organization. A boss with an overwhelming need to be loved may strive to make subordinates loyal to him as an individual. However, this establishes an unstable base for performance. Employees' willingness to work hard will ebb and flow depending upon their current attitude about the boss. Also when this boss leaves the organization, disorganization often follows. The employees' high motivation, which the boss personally inspired, deflates and they do not know what to do (McClellan). Staff members should be motivated by the challenge of achieving the goals of the center, not by the desire to win the approval of the director or to avoid his displeasure.

To encourage the highest level of commitment to the center, the director should seek to involve staff members in setting the goals. By participating in the goal setting process, employees can help shape goals that they personally care about and have a stake in. The more they perceive the center's goals as coinciding with their own professional goals, and the less they perceive them as only the director's goals, the more they will be inclined to work hard toward their accomplishment (McGregor).

#5. Be a Feedback Giver

A Benevolent Boss, who cares primarily about having staff members like her, lavishes praise on them, hoping this will make them feel good about her. A People-Oriented Boss, who cares mainly about stimulating high performance by staff members, provides objective feedback to them, knowing this will help them improve their performance.

Praise, even well-deserved praise, has been shown to have only minimal impact on the long-term performance of workers. Objective feedback, on the other hand, gives them data they can use to change their behavior (Drucker). The more employees know about their own performance, the more they are able to adjust it toward accepted performance standards.

There are several criteria for effective feedback. First and foremost, feedback should focus on facts, not opinions. A director should describe for a teacher exactly how she talks to children and let her draw her own conclusions, rather than offering a judgment about whether her conversational style is good or bad. Making a judgment causes the recipient to react emotionally, either with anger or embarrassment, and obscures the important message.

Feedback should focus on behavior, rather than on the person. A director should report to a teacher that "You spoke rather harshly to the children today," rather than "You are too authoritarian." Talking in terms of personality traits implies inherited constant qualities, which are difficult, if not impossible, to change. Commenting on behavior implies that it is something related to a specific situation that might be changed (Lehner).

Feedback should be timely. The closer feedback is given in time to the point at which the behavior actually occurred, the more likely the recipient will clearly remember the incident and put the information to use (Drucker). If a teacher is told that the children were inattentive when she read to them last week, but she can't remember what she was reading, how she was reading it, or what took place just before the reading, she will not know enough about the incident to change her behavior for the better in the future.

Feedback should be given in frequent small doses. People can absorb only so much feedback at one time and put it to effective use (Lehner).

Feedback in the form of an annual appraisal, which attempts to summarize an entire year's performance in one lump sum, can be overwhelming. Feedback that comes in tiny daily bits is easily digested and put to use.

#6. Be a Delegator

One of the paradoxes of organizational life is that the more authority a boss gives away the more his authority is enhanced (Caplow). Authority can be given away by delegating tasks to subordinates and by granting autonomy to them in the exercise of their day-to-day work.

By assuming greater responsibility within the organization, employees feel more like they are in control of their work and less like puppets on a string. They tend to feel more like they are a significant part of the organization. And they tend to care more about how well the organization performs. The more they respect the organization and care about their performance in it, the more they respect the authority of the leaders of the organization, and the more they value the feedback they receive about their performance from these leaders. As a result, a People-Oriented Boss who grants considerable autonomy to his subordinates is better able to influence their performance.

#7. Be a Facilitator

A People-Oriented Boss facilitates the optimal performance of his subordinates by providing whatever support they need to do their work. This support needs to be provided in a variety of ways. The director needs to provide staff members with the equipment and supplies they require. He needs to ensure that the environment they work in is safe and pleasant. He needs to do all he can to provide them the compensation and benefits they deserve and require.

In addition to providing these basic types of support, a boss needs to be able to support the professional development of staff members. Two ways to do this, which have already been discussed, are granting employees autonomy and providing them with feedback. Another is to provide them with appropriate training opportunities and materials. Finally, a director needs to support the professional development of staff members by being available to listen, to review, to advise, and to counsel. He needs to be a resource of last resort in problem solving. He needs to be a trusted source of expertise. He needs to be able to stimulate people's thinking and self-analysis. In short, he needs to be able to do whatever is needed to facilitate the development and performance of his subordinates.

#8. Be Communicative

That invisible barrier between the boss and her staff tends to play havoc with the flow of communications in a center. A director must be aware of how communications are affected by this barrier in interpreting communications that she receives and in framing messages that she transmits.

One common problem that develops is that directors tend to overrate the effectiveness of downward communications. They become so immersed in all the details of current administrative hassles and crises that they tend to forget who they told about what. After a while they tend to assume that the staff must be aware of what is going on.

More often then not, staff members have only picked up bits and pieces of information about current administrative issues. Having only partial information, the rumor mill tends to fill in the gaps with exaggerated, typically alarmist versions of what is going on. Worse yet, when the data received is sketchy, staff members tend to feel that information is being withheld intentionally. This contributes to undermining the respect for and authority of the director.

Being aware of this scenario, a director should make a regular practice of reporting to staff on the status of current administrative issues. Never assume that subordinates are aware of everything you are,

and never assume that staff members won't be interested in certain issues. In terms of downward communications, it is usually wise to err in the direction of sharing too much rather than keeping employees guessing and grousing.

Upward communications are usually even more sluggish. Information tends to be well filtered before it reaches the director's ears. Since no one wants to be the bearer of bad news, negative information about the organization tends to flow upward much less routinely than does positive information.

Likewise, while personal information and news about staff members tends to flow freely among staff members, it seldom flows upwards. Staff members are often reluctant to share personal information with directors for fear that this information will be held against them in some way.

While a director can do very little to become a part of the center's network of news and gossip, there are specific steps she can take to encourage the upward flow of organizational information. One of the most effective ways is to encourage it by taking action. When a teacher reports a heating problem in her room, take immediate steps to do something about it. When a teacher suggests that one of the center's curriculum goals may be too ambitious, bring this issue up at the next staff meeting to see if there is general agreement about this. If there is, abandon or modify the goal accordingly. The more that staff members see that their input makes a difference, the more they will be willing to share both negative and positive information with the director.

In addition, the director should open multiple channels of upward communication. A director might encourage written or e-mail communications for those times when she is not available or for staff members who may be reluctant to share negative information on a face-to-face basis.

Likewise, the director could reserve time in staff meetings for staff members to report their news and views. Or the director could schedule private talks with individual staff members on a regular basis to discuss their successes, their problems, and their concerns. The more avenues a center provides for communication to take place, the less likely it is that important messages will be withheld or get lost in the cracks.

#9. Be Visible

It is very easy for a director to remove herself from the day-to-day life of the center. Directors spend so much time in meetings, both at the center and away from it, and tend to get so involved in paperwork, e-mail and phone communications that they become invisible to staff members. This pattern can be heightened when a director, in the throws of status anxiety, starts avoiding encounters with staff members who make her feel awkward.

It is often necessary for a director to take deliberate steps to increase her visibility at the center. It may help to set a specific time of the day to take a stroll through the classrooms. A director could from time to time take the opportunity to actually work in the classrooms. When crises erupt in the center, the director should make an immediate appearance and offer whatever leadership or support is needed (Caplow).

#10. Be Open to Feedback

A large measure of a director's status anxiety comes from not knowing how he or she is perceived by subordinates. According to Theodore Caplow, "The usual behavior of a normally ambivalent subordinate is to display his affection and conceal his resentment in the presence of his superior." As a result, a director has a very difficult time getting accurate feedback from the staff on how his performance is perceived and received.

This is a normal situation and should not alarm the director. But she should not allow herself to be lulled into the illusion that she is universally loved (Caplow).

To keep in touch with reality, a director can initiate specific actions to elicit feedback on her performance. She should communicate to staff, both in word and deed, that she welcomes and values their feedback. When staff members offer her negative feedback, she should resist the urge to become defensive. The surest way to discourage honest feedback is to challenge or argue with staff members whenever they deliver painful messages. Listen carefully to what they have to say and then thank them for helping you.

A director can also utilize more formalized procedures for soliciting feedback. In a staff meeting the director can ask staff members to provide anonymous written ratings of her performance. There are a variety of forms that have been developed for this purpose. Or the director can develop her own form. She could ask staff members to rate her performance in areas she identifies on a scale of 1 to 7. By totaling and averaging these ratings she could get an idea of how staff members are perceiving her performance in these areas.

Another approach would be to utilize the critical incidents technique. The director asks staff members to write down two examples of incidents that made them feel good about her performance and two that upset them. By compiling all of these incidents, a director may detect some real patterns — certain things she does that seem to work and others that are causing problems.

A Final Word

In the 1980s a Ken Blanchard sold millions of copies of his book, *The One Minute Manager*. People longed for an easy quick fix to becoming an effective leader. But I am afraid that the path to becoming an effective leader in the early childhood world is not so easy.

Not only does it require the implementation of certain procedures and practices, but it also requires a shift in one's mindset. An effective director needs to understand that she cannot over the long haul improve staff performance through love or fear.   She must believe that staff performance will improve to the extent that they understand and are committed to the goals of the organization and see how their work is connected to the accomplishment of these goals.

References and Resources

Caplow, T. (1976). *How to run any organization.* New York: Holt, Rinehart, and Winston.

Drucker, P. F. (1974). *Management: Tasks, responsibilities, practices.* New York: Harper and Row.

Hackman, J. R., & Suttle, J. L. (1977). *Improving life at work.* Santa Monica, CA: Goodyear Publishing Company.

Lehner, G. F. J. (Summer 1978). "Aids for Giving and Receiving Feedback." *Exchange.*

McClellan, D. C., & Burnham, D. H. (March/April 1976). "Power Is the Great Motivator." *Harvard Business Review.*

McGregor, D. (1960). *The human side of enterprise.* New York: McGraw-Hill Book Company.

Neugebauer, R. (January 1979). "Are You an Effective Leader?" *Exchange.*

Neugebauer, R. (May/June 1982). "Leadership." *Exchange.*

Neugebauer, R. (November 1980). "Make Communications a Two-Way Street." *Exchange.*

Prentice, W. C. H. (September-October 1961). "Understanding Leadership." *Harvard Business Review.*

Rogers, C. (1977). *On personal power.* New York: Dell Publishing Company.

Zaleznik, A. (July/August 1963). "The Human Dilemmas of Leadership." *Harvard Business Review.*

Roger Neugebauer

Roger Neugebauer is publisher of *Exchange Magazine* and a co-founder of the World Forum Foundation.

Heart-centered Leadership

by Nancy Rosenow

Becoming a heart-centered leader is an inside job, and it's not for the faint-of-heart. It's a process of getting to know and accept ourselves so well that nothing outside of us feels threatening anymore. It's making peace with the fears we find in our heart when we get really honest. The classic children's book, *The Velveteen Rabbit* (Williams, 1958), contains a famous paragraph that describes the process perfectly:

You become. It takes a long time.… Generally by the time you are Real, most of your hair has been loved off, and your eyes drop out, and you get loose in the joints and very shabby. But these things don't matter at all, because once you are Real you can't be ugly, except to people who don't understand.

Heart-centered leaders no longer try to cover up their 'realness' for fear of what others will think. They learn to stop judging any parts of themselves as 'ugly.' They move to a place of greater acceptance and love for themselves first, and then for everyone else in their lives.

That all sounds good, but, wow, it's not easy. It's a process, not an event.

It was a revelation to me a few years back when I finally understood that the judgments I feared the most weren't from others, but from myself. I had been living for years as my own worst critic, looking outside myself for acceptance and validation, all the while keeping up an internal dialogue of criticism and judgment. My greatest fear was that others would 'find out' about my flaws and come to the same conclusion I had — that I may not be worthy enough, perfect enough, or good enough to be an effective leader. The irony is that the fear of facing my 'realness' kept me from creating the most real relationships with others. I wasn't able to lead as effectively because my fears got in the way. Only when I began to risk revealing all of me was I able to move into a place where my leadership became more loving, collaborative, and yes, effective.

Author Brene Brown, famous for her TedTalk on vulnerability, has written a wonderful book called *Daring Greatly: How the Courage to Be Vulnerable Transforms the Way We Live, Love, Parent, and Lead* (2012). "Courage starts with showing up and letting ourselves be seen," she writes. That sounds great, but I know how tough it is to really allow myself to be seen. If others truly see me, then they'll notice the parts of me that are "loose in the joints and very shabby" — in a metaphorical sense. (Okay, a little bit in a literal sense, too, since I'm practicing honesty.) It's only when I can move into a place of acceptance and love for all my 'shabby' places that I can be open to real relationships. Because we all have the places inside ourselves we judge as not-good-enough. Much of the hurt in our world comes from trying to hide those places from each other. More connection and meaning and joy is possible as soon as we embrace our 'shabbiness' as an acceptable part of ourselves.

Find Your Kinder Voice

That brings me to what I believe is the first and most important characteristic of a heart-centered leader: the ability to become intentional in our self-acceptance. I've learned to really pay attention to the voice in my head now, asking it to be much kinder. When I hear self-judgment and criticism, I ask myself if I'd want to talk to a friend that way. While the answer is always "of course not," I've really come to understand that the more my self-talk is filled with negativity and criticism, the more likely I am to turn that unkind voice on others, even if I don't mean to. In a school environment, especially, this is a cycle we very much want to break. Consider this: An administrator who is unaware of how self-critical she is passes on her judgmental feelings to the teachers on her staff. The teachers, affected by that negativity, inadvertently pass on those judgmental feelings to their students. And, since we know that the words our children hear from the adults in their lives soon become their own internal voices, the unhealthy cycle lives on in another generation. Or, it stops because we choose to stop it.

Choose Love More Often than Fear

Another vitally important characteristic of a heart-centered leader is the ability to make more choices that are motivated by love instead of fear. Fear and love are always at odds with each other. It's very hard to be truly loving when fear is in control. Almost every day I find myself confronted with the choice to take a deep breath and move through fear into a more loving space, or ride the wave of fear into negativity and doubt. Sometimes, despite my best intentions, fear gets a hold of me and pushes me to the

ground. Then I find myself snapping at others, trying to control the uncontrollable, and making decisions I later regret. When I notice that fear has been pushing me around, I get very still and give myself a big dose of love and self-forgiveness. I remind myself that I am human and fear is part of the human condition, even though it's not as powerful as it would like us to believe. I also remind myself that one of my deepest intentions — not just as a leader, but as a human being — is to operate as much as possible from a place of love and acceptance.

With practice, I have been able to keep fear from controlling me so much. I've learned that fear is quite the liar; it often tries to convince me that I can't take the time for human connection and loving interactions because there's an 'emergency' that's more important, or that 'things will fall apart' if I don't try to exert more control. Over the years, I've started dealing with fear's lies in a gentler way. I treat them like I would a young child… with reassurance and firmness. Often I'll say out loud to myself: "I choose to be loving right now. Love is more powerful than fear."

Believe in Your Own Strength of Heart

For many years, leaders were taught never to appear too emotional. In the past, administrators were often judged as too weak if they ever discussed concepts as 'squishy' as leading in a heart-centered way. Recently, though, this misunderstanding has been turned on its head, as more and more has been written about the need to enlist both head and heart in service to effective leadership. In addition to Brene Brown's work, other popular titles in recent management literature include: *Leadership from the Inside Out: Becoming a Leader for Life* by Kevin Cashman (2008). Heart-centeredness is no longer being judged as weakness, but instead as a source of strength. A new understanding is coming into awareness as leaders increasingly embrace the fact that their effectiveness is grounded in a strong relationship with themselves. The third characteristic vitally important to a heart-centered leader is that she believes in the deep value of her own strength of heart.

A few years ago when I wrote a book about heart-centered teaching, a number of educators contacted me to say I'd touched on a subject they'd been afraid to talk about openly. Many told me they longed for more heart-centered relationships among fellow staff members and with their students, but worried they would be judged harshly if they ever expressed those sentiments. I'd like to think we've now moved into a new era of understanding where no one need apologize ever again for valuing heart-centeredness as a crucial and strong component of effective teaching and leading.

Believe in Everyone's Strength of Heart

Once we as heart-centered leaders have come to accept our own 'Realness,' learned to choose love over fear more often, and come to believe deeply in our strength of heart, then we're ready to support others in doing the same. As we let our staff learn to know more about our 'shabbiness,' we invite others to reveal more of themselves, 'warts and all.' This opens the door to closer connection and keeps people from expending so much energy trying to hide insecurities. With the staff I lead, we have two traditions I value greatly. One is a time when people are invited to tell stories. We choose three names at random each month and those people tell us a story about their 'Realness' in whatever way they choose. There are no rules, no pressure, just an invitation to tell us more about their authentic selves. Over time the stories have become richer and more meaningful as people have 'dared greatly' to 'show up and be seen.'

We also have a tradition of spending some of our staff meetings talking to each other about the 'mistakes' we've made and what we learned from them. As it became more and more acceptable to discuss things that didn't work, it became increasingly obvious that having the courage to 'fail' (by the world's standards) is a prerequisite for doing important work. Heart-centered leaders help others accept

honest mistakes as an important part of a learning orientation to life. It's a joy to work with a staff that has the courage to be 'Real.' No one judges others as 'ugly.' And if that ever happens, the heart-centered leader knows that it's because the person who judges does not yet understand.

Celebrate Often

Heart-centered leaders know they must help set the tone they want in their organizations by focusing more on what's working well than on what's not. Management guru Tom Peters, author of many acclaimed books such as *In Search of Excellence* (Peters & Waterman, 2006) and *The Pursuit of Wow* (1994), has been widely quoted as saying, "Celebrate what you want to see more of." Heart-centered leaders are great celebrators. They rejoice in effort as much as achievement. They notice courage, kindness, commitment, and celebrate those qualities often and exuberantly. They don't wait for the 'big success' to plan a party, for they know that the loving energy people bring to their work is actually more important than any particular achievement.

Organizations led by heart-centered leaders become interdependent, mutually supportive, and joyful. That doesn't mean people don't work hard, get discouraged at times, or face challenges. What it does mean is that any challenge is secondary to the sense of purpose and pleasure felt by a shared commitment to an important mission. Heart-centered leaders feel the mission of the organization deeply and speak of it often. And since each person in the organization is valued for being 'Real,' the mission grows and strengthens as more and more people help define its richness. Work is done with a sense of purpose and dedication to something that transcends each individual. The satisfying feeling of contributing to the greater good flourishes. Now that is something truly worth celebrating.

References

Brown, B. (2012). *Daring greatly: How the courage to be vulnerable transforms the way we live, love, parent, and lead.* New York: Penguin Group.

Cashman, K. (2008). *Leadership from the inside out: Becoming a leader for life.* San Francisco: Berrett Koehler Publishers.

Peters, T., & Waterman, R. (2006). *In search of excellence: Lessons from America's best run companies.* New York: Harper Business.

Peters, T. (1994). *The pursuit of wow!* New York: Vintage Books.

Williams, M. (1958). *The velveteen rabbit.* New York: Doubleday.

Nancy Rosenow

Nancy Rosenow is the executive director of Dimensions Educational Research Foundation/Nature Explore and a founding member of World Forum Foundation's Nature Action Collaborative for Children

Leadership Matters

Creating Anti-bias Change in Early Childhood Programs

by Louise Derman-Sparks, John Nimmo, and Debbie LeeKeenan

"Anti-bias endeavors are part of a proud and long educational tradition — one that continues to seek and to make the dream of justice and equality a reality. It happens day by day, and calls on our best teaching, relationships, and leadership skills."

Derman-Sparks, LeeKeenan, & Nimmo
(2015, p. 164)

An anti-bias approach puts diversity and equity aspirations at the center of all aspects of a program's organization and daily life. This is an activist approach in which children's developing identity, and their questions, observations, and ideas about diversity and bias, shape the education we provide (Derman-Sparks & Edwards, 2010). The program's vision, mission, policies, procedures, learning environment, and curriculum all come into play. In sum, it is a "process, not an event" (Kugelmass, 2004, p. 6), which happens in stages over time.

The leader of an early childhood care and education program plays a central role in cultivating anti-bias education change. She must be intentional and strategic, planning for the long haul — as well as the steps that get a program to its goals. An anti-bias perspective informs everything the leader does. She

also must understand the risks of change, as well as be aware of her own fears, yet not let either the risks or her fears stop one from taking action (Espinosa, 1997). An anti-bias leader must also be willing to deal with complexity. There are no simple answers or quick solutions; there are strategies for dealing with the complexities that emerge when building anti-bias programs.

In this article, we describe some of the key components of effective anti-bias education (ABE) leadership, as well as both the challenges and possibilities.

Create a Culture that Cultivates Staff and Family Commitment, Risk-taking, and Ownership

This work begins with the program leader's first contacts with staff and families and continues on every day of the program. Consider the following strategies:

■ Create a welcoming environment where staff and families feel respected and trusted, free to take risks, and express their feelings and perspectives. Everyone feels supported in their learning, and understands that disequilibrium and discomfort can lead to real growth.

- Provide multiple opportunities for staff and families to regularly, informally and formally, learn about ABE, ask questions, and provide input (e.g. at staff meetings, open houses, parent meetings, informal conversations, and advisory board meetings).

- Generate an ABE mission statement with the staff and with input from families. Begin with visioning: "What would your center look like if it were an excellent anti-bias program?" The mission statement eventually becomes a core theme of a program's operational framework.

- Engage staff in devising, collecting, and analyzing accountability documentation that shows what change is happening and provides the information for planning.

- Model the experience of making changes. Share your challenges, discomforts, and mistakes with your community. Make clear that you also have questions and that you do not know all the answers.

Reading Your Program: A Place to Start

An early childhood program is a complex system of people, relationships, resources, barriers, possibilities, and power dynamics. In order to embark on a strategic process of change, you need to know where the program stands now and what, specifically, you need to shift.

The metaphor of 'reading' the program, adapted from Paulo Freire (1985), stands for the process of gathering and analyzing information related to the changes you want to foster. An initial baseline portrait of the people and various components of your program provides a framework for developing specific strategies to begin working toward your ABE

goals. Consider the following questions (Nimmo, 2011):

- What are the significant contextual factors you need to consider in your center and local community with regard to diversity work (e.g. demographics, politics, history, values, resources)?

- Who are the allies (people who will support you and understand your purpose) you have already identified (e.g. administration, teachers, parents, community members)?

- Who are some potential allies you could reach out to next?

- What resources do you have for your diversity work (e.g. materials for children, classroom arrangements, time for teachers to learn and reflect, commitment from staff, administrators, access to community experts)?

- Who are the gatekeepers in the community? (Who or what can deny or provide access to resources?)

- What barriers do you see to your diversity work (e.g. financial, demographic, education)?

- What fears or concerns do you have about shifting your program to an anti-bias approach?

- What are the three most important long-term goals you have for diversity work at your center?

Considering the assessment above, where do you want to start? What are the specific *strategies/ actions* you can commit to this year (e.g. focus on family inclusion)?

These questions for initially 'reading' your program can also be adapted for documenting and periodically assessing a program's progress in implementing anti-bias education over time.

Foster Anti-bias Educators and Partnerships with Families

The early childhood field recognizes the central importance of professional development and nurturing family partnerships in building quality programs (see Carter & Curtis, 2010). Here we offer a brief summary of specific ABE strategies for this work.

Anti-bias leaders provide the necessary time, space, resources, support, and facilitation for teachers and other staff to be participants in the process of change. They recognize that staff will be on different places in their own anti-bias journeys (Derman-Sparks, & Ramsey, 2011; Tatum, 1992, 1994; Wijeyesinghe & Jackson, 2012). Some may deny noticing differences or having bias themselves or that children have ideas about diversity. Others may be more open to exploring anti-bias issues related to themselves, the children, and the program. Yet others are ready to begin actively implementing ABE. Finally, when a majority of staff makes ABE a part of everything they do, a program reaches the part of the journey where consistent, effective work happens.

The program leader finds ways to provide opportunities that scaffold the learning for all staff. He engages staff in setting objectives for individual, classroom team, and school-wide anti-bias work, makes ABE part of ongoing professional development, supervises, and coaches staff integrating ABE into the daily curriculum, and facilitates staff members' work with families.

Anti-bias efforts also build on families feeling that they belong, the starting point for forming strong, staff/family relationships. These require having an inclusive definition of families and believing in the value of all program members learning from others. The leader works with staff to put into practice a range of anti-bias strategies for family involvement. This includes making sure anti-bias values and goals are transparent to the community, creating family visibility and connection with each other and with staff, and two-way education and dialogue among families and between family and staff. The leader also facilitates problem solving when there is disagreement over anti-bias issues.

Negotiating Conflict

Anti-bias work inevitably generates some disagreement, disequilibrium, and conflicts. These occur when there is cognitive and emotional dissonance between two or more perspectives — whether they are from staff or from families. However, resolving differences in ABE work is not about winners and losers. It is about managing conflict in a way that creates greater equity and inclusion.

If the leader embraces conflict as a key opportunity for creative problem solving, then the outcomes are new insights, perspectives, and behaviors for colleagues, staff, families, and herself. However, fear of conflict can be an obstacle to even embarking on the anti-bias education journey.

Productive handling of differences in a program does *not begin* when an actual conflict occurs. From the beginning, it is about working intentionally and proactively to create a culture and a climate in which disagreement is acceptable, and problem solving supports positive outcomes. It is also essential to recognize that there are no abstract or perfect solutions. Experiencing some ambiguity and uncertainty is inevitable in this process. Rather, look for specific solutions for specific conflict episodes, which make sense in terms of your program's values and context.

We suggest using an approach that we call "Finding the *Third Space*." The third space is the intellectual and emotional place where people in conflict come to a mutually decided agreement that goes beyond their initial viewpoints. Three tactical steps enable people to find the third space in most conflict situations. These are *Acknowledge, Ask, and Adapt* (Derman-Sparks, 2013). The objectives of this sequential process are to devise a solution that works for everyone — at least as much as possible.

Here is an example of using these steps based on a real situation: A child care center serving children from a culture where the infants and toddlers are used to sleeping in hammocks, find that the children will not take naps in the cribs provided by the center (Derman-Sparks, LeeKeenan, & Nimmo, 2015).

Step 1, Acknowledge:

Staff openly recognizes together that a problem exists, as the children are tired, consequently cranky, and easily upset. This problem reflects a clash between the children's home culture and practices with: a) the practices and regulations of centers in the United States, and b) the cultural practices and experiences of the center.

Step 2, Ask:

The center director talks with the families about their children's sleeping habits. She facilitates conversations with the staff, with the objective of gaining clarity about where each person stands on the issues and their desired outcome, and also clarifies her own beliefs and priorities in this particular situation.

Step 3, Adapt:

This is the solution step. The program leader informs staff about what she learned from talking with families and reviews licensing and accreditation requirements. Then she helps them find common ground with the practices of the center, the families, external requirements, and considers alternative ways to solve the problem. Ultimately, the staff agrees to hang hammocks diagonally inside the cribs. They see this solution as satisfying licensing criteria, while also meeting the needs of the infants and toddlers. The solution works with the children.

Leadership Matters

Anti-bias change takes persistence, discipline, energy, and time. An effective leader is intentional and strategic. Everything counts. It is not just what you do, but how you do it.

This work is not without its real challenges. Periods of stagnation, frustration, or feeling out of one's depth do occur. As past directors of early childhood programs, we also understand that you juggle multiple everyday demands. Leaders of anti-bias change need ways to sustain themselves, as well as the people with whom they work. Periodically revisit your vision and hopes for a better world, to remind yourself why you are doing anti-bias work. Regularly acknowledge the program's 'small changes' — the specific anti-bias steps that you, staff, families, and the children have taken, and the resulting growth. Most especially, have a group of supportive colleagues with whom you frequently talk, e-mail, and meet.

Ultimately, it is our lifetime commitment to equity, voice, and social justice that will build early childhood care and education programs where all children and families are visible and thrive.

References and Further Reading

Carter, M., & Curtis, D. (2010). *The visionary director: A handbook for dreaming, organizing, and improvising your center* (2nd edition). St. Paul, MN: Redleaf Press.

Derman-Sparks, L. (2013). Developing culturally responsive caregiving practices. In E. A. Virmani & P. L. Mangione (Eds.), *Infant/toddler caregiving: A guide to culturally sensitive care* (2nd edition) (pp. 68-94). Sacramento, CA: California Department of Education.

Derman-Sparks, L., & Edwards, J. O. (2010). *Anti-bias education for young children and ourselves.* Washington, DC: NAEYC.

Derman-Sparks, L., & Ramsey, P. (2011) *What if all the kids are white?: Anti-bias/multicultural education with young children and families* (2nd edition). New York: Teachers College Press.

Derman-Sparks, L., LeeKeenan, D., & Nimmo, J. (2015). *Leading anti-bias early childhood programs: A guide for change.* New York: Teachers College.

Espinosa, L. (1997). Personal dimensions of leadership. In S. Kagan & B. Bowman (Eds.), *Leadership in early care and education* (pp. 97-104). Washington, DC: NAEYC.

Freire, P. (1985). Reading the world and reading the word: An interview with Paulo Freire. *Language Arts, 62*(1), 15-21.

Kugelmass, J. (2004). T*he inclusive school: Sustaining equity and standards.* New York: Teachers College Press.

Nimmo, J. (2011, November). Anti-bias strategic planning worksheet: Reading your setting to form goals and actions. Unpublished manuscript. Orlando, Florida: NAEYC Annual Conference.

Tatum, B. D. (1994). Teaching white students about racism: The search for white allies and the restoration of hope. *Teachers College Record, 95,* 462-476.

Tatum, B. D. (1992, Spring). Talking about race, learning about racism: The application of racial identity development theory in the classroom. *Harvard Educational Review, 62*(1), 1–24.

Wijeyesinghe, C., & Jackson, III, B. (2012). *New perspectives on racial identity development: Integrating emerging frameworks* (2nd edition). New York: New York University Press.

For a more detailed discussion of the components of anti-bias leadership, as well as the many related issues and strategies, we suggest looking at our book *Leading Anti-bias Early Childhood Programs: A Guide for Change* (Derman-Sparks, LeeKeenan & Nimmo, 2015) and other resources listed at the end of this article.

Louise Derman-Sparks

A Faculty Emeritus of Pacific Oaks College after 33 years of college teaching, Ms. Derman-Sparks previously worked with young children and families as a teacher and director. Co-author of several books, she does keynote presentations, conducts workshops, and consults throughout the United States and internationally. She served on the Governing Board of NAEYC, has been a justice activist for 50 years, and has two grown children, who are human service professionals.

John Nimmo

Dr. Nimmo currently teaches graduate classes for Wheelock College in Singapore and consults on anti-bias education. He was previously associate professor in Family Studies at the University of New Hampshire, where he directed the lab school for a decade. John is the co-author of *Loris Malaguzzi and the Teachers, Leading Anti-bias Early Childhood Programs*, and *Emergent Curriculum* and is collaborating on a video project on children's rights through the World Forum. He holds a doctorate from the University of Massachusetts, and began his teaching career in Australia.

Debbie LeeKeenan

Debbie LeeKeenan is a Visiting Professor in Early Childhood Education at Lesley University in Cambridge, Massachusetts. She was director and lecturer at the Eliot-Pearson Children's School, laboratory school for the Department of Child Study and Human Development at Tufts University from 1996-2013. Past professional experience includes over 40 years of teaching in diverse university, public schools, and early childhood settings. She is a published author in numerous journals and books including *Young Children* and *The Hundred Languages of Children*, first edition. Her most recent book writtenrob with Louise Derman-Sparks and John Nimmo, is *Leading Anti-Bias Early Childhood Programs: A Guide for Change.* Debbie presents at numerous conferences, locally, nationally, and internationally and is a consultant for various school systems and educational organizations.

Effective Leadership Behaviors for Child Care Administrators

Seeking Quality Measurement System Success

by Rachel Robertson

Through the years I have had many opportunities to support programs in various stages of pursuing a quality measurement rating such as NAEYC accreditation, Environmental Rating Scales, or other tools used in Quality Rating and Improvement Systems (QRIS) (collectively known throughout the remainder of this article as quality measurement systems). This privilege has allowed me insight into the strategies and approaches that programs employ to achieve these goals. The good news is that there are many ways to successfully achieve these goals. The bad news is that there is not one simple path to success. However, when reflecting on all of the programs I have worked with, across states, from urban to suburban, from small to large, there are some commonalities in how successful programs pursue a quality measurement system. When considering these common factors, what is most noticeable — and, I propose, a contributing factor to the long-term outcomes — are the characteristics and behaviors of the administrators of successful programs.

Among quality measurement systems, there is no clear description of how administrators are expected to move through the process. This is not necessarily a fault of the systems; it is not their intention to script a program's process. Yes, there are many tasks that are logically the administrator's responsibility — important things that must get done. But there are myriad approaches for how to do this. Sometimes the administrator takes on the process almost completely on his own with staff members only having a vague notion of what the goals of the quality measurement system are. At other times, the program staff are assigned specific roles and tasks and the administrator is largely hands-off. And there are a range of options in between.

The common thread seems to be in the administrator's ability to adopt and employ leadership behaviors and characteristics to not just 'get it done' but to lead her staff and program to success. Many assume that a title or position makes the administrator a leader; that along with learning how to manage the computer systems, the food program, and creating weekly staffing schedules, leadership skills simply develop. But alas, they do not. True, administrators are more naturally inclined to use leadership behaviors, but overall leadership is a learned set of skills. And there is no time more worthwhile to ensure that the administrator of the program understands and implements these characteristics and behaviors than when the program is engaged in an important process like quality measurement and improvement. Following is a description of those leadership characteristics that are essential to this process.

Have a Vision and Share It

There are many reasons a program may be pursuing a quality measurement system:

■ It may want to follow a certain path to high quality.

■ It may be eligible for additional funding if it achieves it.

■ It may desire the marketing advantage.

■ It may have other reasons altogether.

■ It may want to align itself with the standards of a nationally respected early childhood organization.

Whatever her reasons, it is important that the leader can articulate these and that other stakeholders such as staff, families, and the board understand and support them as well.

Consider how pursuing a quality measurement rating fits into overall program goals. Many programs have short-term reasons for pursuing quality measurement systems such as achieving a higher level in a QRIS. This fuels their efforts to achieve the initial endorsement, but what about maintaining those standards over time? It is perfectly acceptable to have short-term goals, but the leader should also ensure that these support the long-term vision for the program. Aligning the program's current efforts with the long-term vision of the program will help staff sustain the high levels of quality achieved during the process, ultimately allowing children, staff, and families to reap the benefits for years to come.

Organization Strategies

Develop systems that will support the process. This should be at the top of your to-do list from the beginning. Creating tools as you go along can hamper the process and make the effort feel disjointed. Spending time on the front end thinking through your organization's needs will pay off in the long run.

Make sure everyone knows the goals, timeline, tasks, and expectations involved. Designate a time and place to share information, expectations, and updates. Consider methods of keeping both staff and families informed.

Read the materials provided about the quality measurement system. Each system has specific structural components, paperwork expectations, deadlines, and process tools. It is important to understand all of these before diving in.

Set Effective Short- and Long-range Goals

Have high expectations. Identify what your expectations are. Write them out and be sure you understand them and have aligned them with your vision for your program. Then share them. Make sure you are very clear about what you expect from your staffing team (including yourself) and don't hesitate to tell them. From "expecting every staff person to fully participate in the quality measurement process" to "expecting everyone to accomplish their action plans on time," your expectations will set a standard and hold staff accountable.

Set small goals. Identifying how each staff member and classroom needs to improve, developing achievable and realistic goals, providing the support staff needed to achieve goals, and monitoring progress are all important aspects of the process. Breaking tasks into small achievable goals will help everyone meet your expectations and realize the vision.

Follow the SMART goal method: specific, measurable, achievable, realistic, and time-bound. "Clean the classroom" is not a SMART goal. Staff assigned to this task won't know what 'clean' means to the director, there is no deadline, and it may not be realistic if there is no support or time allotted for the task. "Scrub each classroom shelf and re-label shelves and bins by October 10" is a SMART goal.

Delegate. This means allowing staff the opportunity to contribute, to play a part in a collaboration, and to develop professionally. But delegation doesn't mean assigning a task and then forgetting about it — or checking it off a to-do list; a manager must still follow-up on delegated tasks as she would with any other goals.

Manage the Change Process

Pursuing a quality measurement system process means initiating change in some or many parts of your program. Although it is good change (based on the standards of the system), this doesn't mean it will be easy for your staff. Understanding varying perspectives and being prepared for objections to proposed changes is important. For example, changing a lesson plan may cause a teacher to feel judged, like he has been doing it wrong. As a result, he may feel offended. This is surely not the intended message, but it is a common response to change. Here are some ways to make change go more smoothly:

Involve staff in the change. Let them discover new ways to improve their teaching, increase their skills, and ensure optimal development and care for children. Choosing to change is easier than being told to change. Plus, you'll all benefit from the great ideas likely to be generated by multiple staff members.

Be enthusiastic about the process (hard work and all). Being a champion and cheerleader on both easy days and hard days is an often overlooked priority for program leaders. It seems simple, but it is very important. If the administrator can remain positive and committed, the staff will follow her lead.

Prioritize Professional Development for Staff

Consider the proverb "Give a man a fish, and you feed him for a day. Teach him to fish, and you feed him for a lifetime." Leaders need to allow staff to grow, develop, evolve, try, fail, and try again. Any boss can tell people what to do. Leaders support the professionals they work with and encourage them to reach their potential and meet their own goals, as well as those of the program. Leaders celebrate both successes and challenges, keeping the big picture and long-term vision in focus at all times.

One way to help engage staff is to develop individual professional development plans for all staff members. Whether required by the quality measurement system or not, this is an important practice. Setting goals and focusing on the professional growth of each individual staff member will ensure every person receives the attention they need to flourish and the training or education that best meets their needs. Focus on training and education. With the increased focus, and in some cases requirements, on staff educational qualifications in the past few years, many are equating professional development with "going back to school." For some staff this may be a worthwhile and realistic goal, for others it may not be. Either way, professional development includes training, classroom mentoring, coaching, and more. As a leader, it is essential to tailor all professional development to the needs of individual staff members and not focus solely on one type or activity.

While other leadership characteristics are effective, these leadership characteristics and behaviors are essential to success. They will surely increase a program's odds as they pursue a quality measurement system, and will also contribute to the growth and development of the program and staff overall.

Maintain Your Achievement

Programs typically spend one year or more pursuing a quality measurement system. Once they achieve this important goal and no longer have a visit or assessment looming in the future, they are often unsure of what to focus on next. But the truth is the work has only just begun. The most challenging part of quality measurement systems is maintaining the standards over time. Luckily, the same leadership characteristics that allowed you to achieve quality measurement system success will also prove useful in the following years as you commit to maintaining or increasing the level of high quality your program has achieved. It is easy to slip back into old behaviors once the pressure is off. However, it is essential not to make this mistake. Take time to celebrate your achievement and then begin the next round of goal-setting, professional development planning, and quality improvement.

Adopting these leadership skills takes effort, but they will no doubt make you a leader others want to follow and learn from, and ensure that your program is truly one of the best, offering experiences for children that will impact them for a lifetime.

Resource

You can read more about effective leadership characteristics, professional development, change management, and other essential tips and tools for quality measurement system success in *Prove It! Achieving Recognition for Your Early Childhood Program* by Rachel Robertson and Miriam Dressler (Redleaf Press, 2009).

Rachel Robertson

Rachel Robertson, Vice President of Learning & Development, has had the privilege of teaching young children and the adults who work with them for over 20 years. She is the author of numerous articles and books, including the *Deployment Journal Series* (Elva Resa), *Prove It: Achieving Quality Recognition for Your Early Childhood Program and Healthy Children, Healthy Lives, A Teacher's Promise* (August 2015 release), and *When You Just Have to Roar* (Redleaf Press). She is currently the Senior Director of Education and Development for Bright Horizons Family Solutions.

The Role of Knowledge in Leadership

by Maurice Sykes

To be a successful leader in early childhood education, you must be a seeker and a distributor of knowledge. The seeking of knowledge is driven by one key element: curiosity. Curiosity sounds simple, but the power in this one small concept knows no bounds. In curiosity we find the catalyst that has spurred the discovery and the growth of knowledge throughout all of human history. The children whose lives we seek to enrich are already in touch with this incredible learning tool. Anyone who has worked with young children knows that you cannot leave them in a room with a pile of blocks without witnessing curiosity manifesting itself. At once, the questions come to life:

■ What designs can be pieced together out of these blocks?

■ What structures can be made?

■ How high can the blocks be stacked before they topple over?

Children's natural curiosity propels them to discover the answers to these questions. What started out as a pile of unremarkable blocks suddenly increases one hundredfold in value. Why? Because blocks on their own are just blocks. But blocks mixed with curiosity yield a far greater treasure: knowledge.

Leaders in early childhood education should take their cues from how children construct knowledge. Children are naturally curious about everything around them. They have theories and hypotheses that they are constantly testing through exploration and experimentation. Blocks may look different to us than they do to children, but we can learn much from children's curiosity that can be brought into our own lives. Curiosity about the way we work and teach will lead to experimentation. Experimentation will lead to innovation, and innovation can lead to new and powerful discoveries.

Knowledge is not a passive ideal. It is not a lofty, academic concept. It is practical, it is hands-on, and it is accessible to anyone, of any age, who chooses to engage in the joy of discovery, the joy of personal and intellectual renewal, and the joy of understanding that knowledge is power. It is up to us to create an environment — for children and adults — where the pursuit of knowledge is encouraged, honored, and celebrated.

The Knowledge Economy

People in our global society are constantly in search of knowledge, because knowledge is power. Experts are sought in every field to promote and advance knowledge. Geopolitical barriers have crumbled, giving us international access to people and ideas that are turning impossibilities into possibilities that we never dreamed of before. The 'knowledge economy' goes beyond our old ways of doing things. It seeks to apply new skills and discoveries to how things work in the world — all through the vehicle of expanding knowledge.

As educators, we have a key part to play in this ever-evolving global network of knowledge. It is our responsibility to ensure that the children in our care exit our programs with the skills, knowledge, and dispositions they need to be successful. The responsibility for creating appropriate learning experiences that will enable them to do this lies in our hands.

The leader's role in the knowledge arena is not to establish a culture where "everything goes." We should not be interested in knowledge for knowledge's sake. A successful leader understands that knowledge is a tool — one that, in our field, will enable us to further the aim of enriching the lives of young children.

Knowledge is exchangeable, knowledge is transportable, and knowledge is in demand. It is our responsibility as leaders in early childhood education to see that the seeds of knowledge are planted early and sustained. To ensure that this takes place, we must familiarize ourselves with knowledge on four levels: knowledge of self, knowledge of others, knowledge of craft, and knowledge of leadership.

Knowledge of Self

A leader who has not developed self-knowledge cannot perform his or her role effectively. The reason for this is simple. If you do not know who *you* are and what makes you tick, it's hard to know where you are going, let alone how to lead others toward achieving *their* personal best. Every strong house is built upon a strong foundation. For a leader, that foundation is possessing self-knowledge and clarity about your personal core values.

Cultivating an awareness of who you are and how you operate in multiple arenas is critical to developing effective leadership. Self-knowledge is not just about what you know. It is also about understanding what you don't know. Ask yourself:

- Who am I?

- Why am I here?

- What am I good at?

- What difference do I plan to make in this world?

- How do others see me?

- What is my leadership style?

- What is my strongest belief, that thing that motivates my every action?

Only after you engage in this task of self-exploration can you begin to use your personal strengths and self-confidence to foster self-knowledge in others.

To have self-knowledge is to be filled with wonder, adventure, curiosity, and creativity. We must understand the importance of this concept if we are to be successful as leaders. Leaders who have a good and realistic sense of self will instill confidence in those they lead and inspire them to do their personal best for the organization and for the children and families they serve.

Knowledge of Others

In addition to having self-knowledge, it is equally as important to have knowledge of the people you lead. A leader must engage in understanding the knowledge, skills, and temperaments of his or her team members and then must use that knowledge to inspire and maximize performance. This can be done through informal assessments, casual observations, inventories such as multiple intelligences questionnaires, learning style assessments, or more formalized assessment tools like the Myers-Briggs Type Indicator. Whatever method you use, it is important to develop a way of knowing your followers so you can adjust your leadership approach to each person.

This does not mean that you are constantly changing your style to suit the idiosyncrasies of each individual; however, it does acknowledge that you know that adults, just like children, are not all the same and that one's leadership style does not fit all.

The best way to gain knowledge of others is by wandering around listening and observing. That means that you need to come out of your office and go into classrooms as a matter of daily practice. Talk to the children and observe firsthand the challenges they and the staff face. Then, when you talk to the teachers about their teaching practices, you will be talking from a more authentic perspective.

Other ways of increasing your knowledge of others is through informal one-on-one conversations, where you get to learn things about the person's hopes, dreams, and aspirations. You might ask them:

■ How do you prefer to do your work?

■ How do you prefer to receive feedback and general communication?

■ How do you like to be recognized and rewarded?

■ What can I do to make your job more manageable and enjoyable?

Knowledge of Craft

Craft knowledge, or 'wisdom of craft,' is the wealth of teaching knowledge that very skilled practitioners know and understand about their own practice. It is also the knowledge base about teaching and learning that effective leaders must have in order to lead an early learning community. The people that you lead must believe that you know what you are talking about and that your knowledge base comes from a rich blend of experience, research, and practice.

Early in the movement toward state content standards, teacher educators would often say about teachers' lack of craft knowledge, "You can't teach that which you do not know." Well, the same holds true for leaders: you can't lead on that which you have not experienced. It is important that leaders have experiential knowledge, as well as theoretical knowledge about teaching young children. We must know and understand how to translate the principles of child development into a developmentally appropriate pedagogy of child development.

Effective leaders must acquire the knowledge and skills they need to establish and maintain a community of professional practice — one that is committed to a process of continual inquiry, reflection, experimentation, and research in order to improve teaching practice.

Knowledge of Leadership

Effective leaders are always in search of new opportunities to sharpen their mental 'saws' (Stephen Covey's term) and deepen their understanding of the art and science of leadership. They achieve this through the acquisition of new skills, new knowledge, and new perspectives. Leaders who continue to expand their repertoire of skills throughout their careers are more likely to be successful. Too often, leaders are so consumed with the development of others that they forget that they have an obligation to themselves, and to those they lead, to continue to grow, stretch, and evolve as leaders.

It is critical that leaders tend to their own professional growth and development by continuing to enhance and refine their repertoire of leadership skills and knowledge throughout their professional careers. It all begins with the leader's personalized professional growth plan (PPGP). Your PPGP is your road map for where you are going and how you plan to get there. Use it to take stock of what you already know about leadership and which aspects of leadership you desire to know more about. Ask yourself:

■ What are my strengths, and how can I play to them?

■ What are some developmental experiences that I could assign to myself to gain new knowledge?

■ Where are the arenas of opportunity, within my own bailiwick, in which I can stretch and grow as a leader, and learn something new?

A great deal of leadership development comes as a result of reflection on everyday occurrences. Reflection is part of the knowledge-seeking journey. When you take the time to stop and reflect, new insights may be revealed for old problems. You can draw on this new learning from past experiences and apply it to experiences in the future.

Leaders should seek new challenges inside and outside their organizations that will allow them to build on their current leadership skill set. For example, perhaps you want to try your hand at applying the situational leadership framework to an individual or a group. Or maybe you want to know more about creating professional learning communities. Regardless of your learning goals, you must have a platform for yourself that is built around a certain set of thoughtful questions:

■ What do I already know, and what am I already able to do as a leader?

■ What do I want to know more about?

■ How, and in what settings, do I want to learn?

■ What internal and external developmental assignments will help me learn more about leadership?

■ How will I measure my success at becoming more knowledgeable about leadership?

■ How will I use the knowledge I seek to do the right thing for children and families?

Conclusion

As a leader, you must develop the habit of mind that seeks to understand the dynamic of what is going on around you. This, above all else, will help you to create the knowledge-based culture that is the foundation for successful leadership in early childhood education. This leadership will in turn ultimately help you do the right thing for the children themselves.

References

Covey, S. (1990). *The 7 habits of highly effective people.* New York: Simon & Schuster.

Maurice Sykes

Maurice Sykes is the director of the Early Childhood Leadership Institute at the University of the District of Columbia's National Center for Urban Education. This article is adapted from the "Knowledge" chapter of his book *Doing the Right Thing for Children: Eight Qualities of Leadership* (Redleaf Press, 2014).

Spreading the Wealth: Leadership at All Levels

by Debra R. Sullivan

I've said it often: To children, all grown-ups are leaders and all grown-ups are teachers. Young children do not make such fine distinctions between the various positions individuals hold in our programs. The lead teacher, the assistant, the custodian, the cook, the director — whatever your role, young children see all grown-ups as 'the people in charge.' It is up to us to 'spread the wealth' and pay attention to how all leadership is expected, supported, experienced, accessible, and noticed at every level and in every position.

To prepare for this article, I had discussions with center directors from around the country. Eight questions emerged from these discussions, which I will address in the balance of the article.

Emerging Questions about Leadership

Eight questions emerged during our discussion:

■ Must leaders be administrators?

■ How do we delegate leadership in a way that communicates that everyone is a leader, organizational leadership is broad and deep, and people can have time away without worry?

■ What characterizes a leader who can form an effective team that functions well in his/her absence?

■ How do we cultivate leadership skills in our teachers who aspire to a director position?

■ How do we motivate staff to grow professionally?

■ How do we help teachers shift their perspective so that leadership occurs almost naturally or they come to it with guidance, but through their own realization?

■ How do we provide effective training that brings out responsibility and leadership potential in each person?

■ What are some 'Next Steps' for encouraging leadership at all levels in our organizations?

Question 1:
Must leaders be administrators?

My first reaction to this question is, "Absolutely not!!" To serve as a visionary and team leader, to hold responsibility for a program's long-term mission and strategic direction, a leader needs strong leadership ability at the moment administrative leadership is appointed. And most administrators develop leadership skills over time. When staff can demonstrate leadership at any level within our programs, they have opportunities to hone their special skills and abilities so that 'tried' and true' leadership can emerge when they assume an administrative position. If we wait until people take on administrative positions to begin practicing leadership, we may well be setting them up for failure. Pay attention to leadership wherever it shows up and you will be surprised at how much leadership you already have available for your use.

Question 2:
How do we delegate leadership in a way that communicates that everyone is a leader, organizational leadership is broad and deep, and people can have time away without worry?

When we consider delegating leadership, we must revisit the concept of abundance thinking shared in my last article on mentoring. Delegating leadership means sharing leadership — stepping aside or stepping back to leave room for someone else to step up. At what point do 'leaders' decide that leadership can be demonstrated by anyone 'up and down the line'? Delegating leadership means moving to the position of follower so that another can lead. Spreading leadership broad and deep results in a more inclusive process that represents everyone and provides the leader with the opportunity to:

1) not worry.

2) not have to be in charge of everything.

3) not have to work alone.

4) begin to recognize, appreciate, support, and make use of the leadership potential of those who surround us (very important).

Question 3:
What characterizes a leader who can form an effective team that functions well in his/her absence?

Actually, the answer to this question is quite easy. A leader who can form an effective team is very intentional about creating replacement leadership. If I want my program to function well in my absence, I put people in place who can do whatever I can do and who can also do whatever I can't do. This is similar to what I have said about mentoring: We have to be willing to grow our own replacements, whether they be temporary replacements to cover our absences or permanent replacements when we move on or retire.

Question 4:
How do we cultivate leadership skills in our teachers who aspire to a director position?

It is true that different skills and traits are required of teachers and directors, but that does not mean that one person cannot possess both. A popular question that arises in the leadership literature is whether leaders are born or made — and my answer is, "Both." All of us have leadership ability that combines innate characteristics and skills we have honed over time.

In our programs, we may well have great teachers who possess the skills needed to serve as director. Those skills and abilities may be apparent early on or they may be in an incubational stage that requires your attention, care, and support. In either event, you can best develop the skills of your great teachers by recognizing their unique and individual potential and providing opportunities for that potential to flourish, mature, and expand.

Question 5:
How do we motivate staff to grow professionally?

In our discussions, one director quoted Piaget as having said, "You don't learn something until you see a need to know it." The concept of motivation — extrinsic and intrinsic — fits in here. Extrinsic motivation is when individuals are motivated by the need to receive rewards or punishments to alter their behavior. Intrinsic motivation is when an individual's behavior arises from his or her own needs, not how others will respond. To motivate staff extrinsically, you need only to know what reward or punishment will make them do as you wish. To motivate staff to grow intrinsically, as with mentoring, you must first know what individuals want for themselves and for their future. Motivation occurs when a staff member sees a future possibility and wants to get there. We work really hard to get what we want.

If you want to grow more leadership by helping teachers see themselves as directors, then you have to let teachers know that you support the development of their leadership skills. Your cook may want to move into a teaching position. He or she will be motivated to learn more about teaching methods and child development. Lead teachers may want to closely examine their teaching skill and develop their abilities to manage the responsibilities of a master teacher. He or she will be motivated to learn more about curriculum development and implementation. Whenever you want to motivate your staff, help them get where they really want to go. You will find that motivating them to grow professionally will be surprisingly easy.

Question 6:
How do we help teachers shift their perspective so that leadership occurs almost naturally or they come to it with guidance, but through their own realization?

Natural leadership occurs when people are provided with opportunities to do what they do best. It may be a two-prong matter of shifting teachers' perspectives and the perspectives of their supervisors. To begin, all of us serve as both leaders and followers. From our positions as followers, we can benefit from reflection on our own leadership strengths and how we can contribute more to the leadership process. From our position as leaders, we need to take a step back so that others can take advantage of leadership opportunities.

Many people may be good at what they do, but leaders do what they are good at. When we have the

opportunity to do what we are good at, we realize our own leadership potential and our own role in the leadership process. All it takes is one good leadership opportunity and the accolades will roll in. After that, just try to shift an emerging leader back to a position as follower!

Question 7:
How do we provide effective training that brings out responsibility and leadership potential in each person?

The most effective training for bringing out responsibility and leadership potential begins with those who supervise others. It can be a challenge to act responsibly and engage in leadership if you are not provided the opportunity to do so. Responsibility in the workplace happens when we think we have some control over our work. Leadership potential emerges when others recognize, support, and make space for our unique gifts, strengths, and contributions to the workplace. Directors, lead teachers, mentors, and coaches must be intentional about providing others with many opportunities to learn about leadership and demonstrate responsibility. We know that children need access and exposure to an abundance of rich, stimulating experiences that include just enough disequilibrium to generate new learning. We don't lose that need just because we grow up. As adults, we need these experiences and we need to provide these for others.

It's about giving up tight control and creating an environment in the workplace that empowers everyone. I visit many programs where curriculum is 'teacher-proof' and there is a strict procedure and process for every aspect of the work. These organizations create a climate where there is no need to think — just follow the highly-scripted directions. Such environments leave little room for responsibility and leadership. Effective training involves leaders stepping back, letting others step up, letting go, and letting leadership happen.

Question 8:
What are some 'Next Steps' we can take to encourage leadership at all levels in our programs?

We can start by truly believing that leadership can, does, and should exist at all levels and with every person in our organizations. When we operate under the assumption that "if you want something done right, you have to do it yourself," we inevitably create environments in which few have the opportunity to demonstrate leadership and even fewer have the opportunity to participate in the leadership process. 'Hoarding' leadership never produces more leadership and can even harm our programs because it is an extremely rare individual who has the ability to run a highly successful program alone. Listed are some more 'next steps':

- Leadership can emerge anywhere. Keep your eyes open!

- Provide opportunities for people to practice leadership. Don't be in charge of everything. Anytime is a good time to hone your own ability to be a good follower.

- Everyone should be in charge of at least one thing. It can be large or small, but if leadership is to live at every level, there should be a leadership opportunity at every level.

- Expect leadership from every member of your staff. People often rise to the level that is expected of them. If you do not expect leadership, you probably won't find it.

- Create a work environment where it's okay to make mistakes. Naturally, I'm not talking about costly mistakes or unsafe practices. I'm talking about allowing others to try something new. We expect children to try what is new. It's part of the learning process for adults as well.

- Learn about everyone's unique gifts, strengths, and contributions and find a place for these in the leadership process. If you don't know, find out.

- Remember that responsibility must come with a big dose of leadership. To have responsibility without the ability to influence process or product is just more work.

- Remember that you are not indispensible! We all want to be, but that is just not possible.

In Conclusion

Spreading the wealth means letting go of our own version of perfection and letting another version emerge. It is about creating, supporting, and maintaining an environment in which emerging leaders can have the confidence and support necessary to demonstrate leadership and experience success.

Debra Ren-Etta Sullivan

Debra Ren-Etta Sullivan is the cofounder and president of the Praxis Institute for Early Childhood Education — a new, racially, culturally, and linguistically diverse college that provides graduate and undergraduate education and professional development for people who work with young children. Prior to beginning the Praxis Institute, she served six years as the dean at Pacific Oaks College Northwest. Dr. Sullivan has worked in higher education for the last 23 years as a teacher, researcher, curriculum developer, and administrator. She earned her doctorate in educational leadership and her master's degree in curriculum and instruction from Seattle University. Currently, Dr. Sullivan serves on Washington State's Early Learning Council, the Foundation for Early Learning Advisory, the Families and Education Levy Oversight Committee, the National Association for the Education of Young Children Professional Development review panel and nominating panel, and the *ParentMap Magazine* editorial board. Publications include *Learning to Lead: Effective Leadership Skills for Teachers of Young Children* (Redleaf Press, 2003). Dr. Sullivan teaches undergraduate and graduate-level leadership classes and has over 10 years of experience providing consultation, workshops, presentations, and addresses on topics such as leadership development, cultural relevancy, organizational change, and school readiness.

So You're a Director

What Else Can Go Wrong?

by Roger Neugebauer

Life is like that sometimes. You knock yourself out to rise to the top of your profession as a child care center director or owner, and what do you get — teachers calling in sick at 6:30 am, a playground degenerating into a mud puddle, late parents, red ink in the checkbook, intransigent licensing officials... the whole litany of daily headaches.

But these are just the pesky, garden variety problems. What every director must be prepared for are the fatal follies — the five pitfalls that plague leaders in early childhood education:

Pitfall #1:
Legend in Your Own Mind

Just beneath the surface of nearly every director is an ego struggling to control everything that goes on. Not that directors don't know intellectually that they should share responsibilities. It's just that emotionally they can't let go.

Delegation means never having to say you're worried. But it is very difficult for a director to delegate a task and not worry that it will be done right. It requires a deliberate effort to develop trust in your subordinates, to accept that subordinates will do things differently, and to allow them to make mistakes along the way.

A refusal to let go can have serious consequences. In the short term, it can undermine staff motivation. Staff members will be frustrated when they are not trusted to share responsibilities.

In the long term, it can undermine the future of the organization. In a non profit center, where the organization will outlive the director, failure to develop a strong management team can leave the center in chaos when a director leaves. In a for profit center, it can handicap the sale of the business. According to acquisition expert Lisa Berger, buyers of businesses "look for companies showing management depth that can generate profits without their master architects."

It takes a person with a great deal of self-confidence to put up with the plethora of aggravations and the paucity of rewards from running a child care center. But the real challenge for a director is to keep one's ego in check. Your goal as a director should be to work yourself out of a job — to build up a team that can run the organization without you.

Pitfall #2:
Things That Go Bump in the Night

A common failing of child care organizations is to let changes in consumer attitudes; changes in employment trends; changes in funding, financing, or regulatory patterns; and changes in the competition sneak up on you. Regis McKenna, the marketing guru who put Silicon Valley on the map, calls these unanticipated events "things that go bump in the night." Organizations don't see them coming; but, like the iceberg that sank the Titanic, they can do a lot of damage.

Child care centers are not islands onto themselves. They are increasingly influenced by the forces shaping society at-large —the ups and downs of the insurance industry, concerns over the federal deficit, the barbs of the 'pro family' movement, the ebbs and flows of various types of businesses, competition from Japan and Korea, and fears of AIDS. Many non profit child care programs were forced to close their doors when they failed to prepare for the dramatic funding cuts promised and carried out by Ronald Reagan. Likewise, a number of mid-size for profit child care chains launched ambitious growth plans in the mid 1980s, which went sour because the companies had failed to take seriously warnings about the staffing shortage.

Small business consultant Gary Goldstick advises, "No matter how committed they are to developing their businesses, managers must allocate 10% to 20% of their time to reading trade journals, the *Wall Street Journal*, and to attending industry trade shows."

Child care owners and directors would be well advised to set time aside to read *American Demographics* and *Young Children* in addition to *Exchange*, to track the progress of the ABC Bill as closely as they track the social development of Sammy or Sarah, to attend meetings of the Chamber of Commerce as well as their local directors' group. By failing to keep in touch with the world outside the center, a director is failing the center.

Pitfall #3:
The Disney World School of Management

A director can also fall into the trap of managing with her eyes closed to problems within the organization. When serious problems are developing, it is sometimes tempting to put blinders on and pretend they don't exist, to operate in a child care Fantasyland.

Center director Olson found himself having to aggressively juggle payables and receivables at the end of every month. He told himself that this was just a temporary cash flow problem. When confronted directly by his banker with the center's poor financial performance over the past year, he explained the problems away with a web of rationalizations.

Deep down inside, of course, he sensed that the center was in serious trouble. But by refusing to see the problem, he was trying to avoid having to deal with it. He was deluding himself, and digging his center deeper and deeper into a hole.

Successful directors keep their fingers on the pulse of the organization. They have in place effective financial, marketing, and programmatic controls so that potential problems can be flagged before they get out of hand. They stay involved with the day-to-day activities of the organization. They solicit feedback from staff and complaints from parents.

Most importantly, successful directors have the courage to act. They are willing to face up to problems and to admit to mistakes. They know when to cut their losses and when to seek dramatic remedies.

Pitfall #4:
When You're Down, You're Down

Who can forget that wrenching scene in the Los Angeles Olympics when the Swiss runner staggered to the finish line of the women's marathon barely able to control her legs. Her body had exerted its last ounce of energy, but she was able to finish the race on sheer willpower.

Athletics abounds with stories of such grit and determination. A standard maxim of coaches is "Ya Gotta Wanna." In fact, analysts often observe that success in athletics is 75% psychological and 25% physical.

Center directors need the same level of tenacity. They are frequently confronted by obstacles which, if not physically painful, are as mentally and emotionally demanding as any marathon effort.

Yet, there are seldom 100,000 fans sitting around the office cheering on a director struggling with a deepening cash flow crisis. There are many times every week when it would be so easy for a director to throw up her hands in frustration and quit. What separates those directors who do quit and those who make it, more often than not, is mental toughness-the ability to withstand tremendous stress and maintain a forward motion.

Pitfall #5:
When You're Up, You're Down

Now the really bad news. Not only can crises drive a director out of business, so can success.

Every week the *Wall Street Journal* will document the story of some small enterprise that struggled for years on a shoestring, became a resounding success, and then fell apart. What typically happens is that the company is unprepared for success.

A new, emerging business can survive on the hard work of one person handling all the management tasks and usually does. But as the business grows, this one person is stretched too far. She can't attend to all the details as before, and the business begins to suffer.

Such a boom and bust cycle can occur in the child care world as well. A successful, growing child care business needs to be planning ahead for success — setting up administrative systems to handle increased workload, developing quality control procedures to ensure that services do not slip, and rethinking the organizational structure to keep tasks clearly and appropriately assigned.

In addition, as your organization grows, you need to have a long range plan in place. Such a plan can help direct your energies and ensure that your growth is logical and not haphazard.

Roger Neugebauer

Roger Neugebauer is publisher of *Exchange Magazine* and a co-founder of the World Forum Foundation.

The Art of Leadership

What We've Learned in 38 Years

by Bonnie Neugebauer and Roger Neugebauer

We have had the opportunity to work with thousands of center directors around the world for the past four decades. Lucky us! Not only has this built our profound respect for the amazing work we observe, but it has also given us the opportunity to make some off-the-beaten-path observations about leadership in the early care and education arena.

Life on the Ground is Not Like the Leadership Textbooks Describe

This observation is a bit like what Mark McCormack conveyed in *What They Don't Teach You at Harvard Business School* (1986) with a bit less glamour. In many early childhood leadership textbooks, problems faced by center directors can often be solved with a clever application of logic and hard work.

■ Have an under-performing staff member? Well, take these three actions and the problem will go away.

■ Have a parent who is a chronic complainer? Here is what you say.

■ Have a cash flow crisis? Then you adjust this, increase that, and apply for something else and — *Presto Change-o!* — you are back in business.

In real life in a center, the underperforming staff member, the nagging parent, and the cash flow crisis all hit at the same time. Meanwhile, you are scheduled for an annual licensing inspection in two days. Plus, the roof is leaking, again.

Challenges can seldom be addressed with straight-line solutions. And most solutions beget other challenges: if you raise fees to help with cash flow, three families take their kids to less expensive centers. If you assuage the parent whose child has been bitten, you anger the parent of the biter. If you fire the underperforming staff member, all her friends on staff are now disgruntled. And so on.

As much as any new or about-to-be director needs some good education and some handy resource books, what you really need is a confidante — a mentor. Every new director needs an experienced director to call on when things get out of hand, as well as to celebrate with when things go well. As the Rolling Stones observed in "Let it Bleed":

Well, we all need someone

we can lean on

And if you want it,

you can lean on me.

Pick Your Staff Wisely

In the National Football League, the annual draft has become nearly as big a sensation as the Super Bowl. Professional football teams sink or swim based primarily on how good a job they do in analyzing talent to select in the draft. Teams can go from humdrum to top-notch with two good drafts (just check out the Seattle Seahawks).

Child care centers will never get all the glory of Super Bowl champions, but the impact of their staff selection is more dramatic. If you put together an all-star team of teachers, your center can become a stimulating place for children and families, and your life as a director can be a very enjoyable experience. A team of so-so teachers results in a program that is okay but not great, where parents are uninvolved and unexcited, and where the director's job of trying to make lemonade out of lemons is very stressful.

With all the financial and organizational pressures on centers, it is often hard to find the time or energy to invest in a first-class selection process when an opening occurs. There is the temptation to hire the first warm body that comes through the door. But in the big picture, any extra time and patience spent in finding the right person pays huge dividends. And, just as importantly, when you have that all-star team in place, make sure you toot your own horn so that all great teachers entering the field want to join your team.

Relationships Matter

In one of the most meaningful articles in the 38-year history of *Exchange*, Ashley Montagu (1995) observed...

"The principal qualification for an early childhood teacher should be the ability to love. This requirement should stand above all others. A teacher of young children, more than anything else, must be able to love children unconditionally, to be able to communicate to them, without any patronizing and without any strings attached, that she is their friend — for friendship, it must be understood, is just another word for love.

"Early childhood educators are the unacknowledged legislators of the world. By befriending children they care for, they teach children how to be friends, how to be deeply involved in the welfare of others. By sharing their commitment to friendship with parents — in a non-threatening, non-patronizing manner — they can help parents see the value of providing a loving environment in the home."

Early childhood programs are under tremendous pressure to deliver children to public schools who are proficient in reading, writing, and arithmetic. This pressure flies in the face of all research... and common sense... that tells us that children need to have unpressured childhoods, that the most important achievement for preschool children is to develop their social skills — to experience the joy of having friends and to learn how to be a friend. Standing tall in defense of friendship is a significant priority for early childhood leaders.

You Need to Keep Your Eyes Focused Outside as Much as Inside

Paying attention to all the internal intricacies of keeping a center on track certainly demands a lot of a director's attention. But while you are focusing on all these internal dynamics, the world outside is not sitting still.

It's an overused axiom that the pace of change is increasing all the time and it's easy to be overwhelmed by it: a major industry in town on the verge of going out of existence, a local Pre-K initiative being touted by the mayor that may lure many of your customers away, a new center down the street that is gaining tons of attention with its "iPad for every child" promotion, new regulations about how food is to be prepared, and a prominent local businessperson promoting the value of early academics. But each of these developments can have as much impact on the future of your center as a leaky toilet or a no-show toddler teacher. Early childhood programs are no longer innocent little classrooms where life goes on, oblivious to the outside world. Today our programs are an integral part of bigger social systems. They impact these systems — shaping the workforce and citizenry of the future — and are impacted by them: economics, politics, technology, and even climate change.

We're All in this Together

Before we started *Exchange*, we quit our jobs and spent 10 months touring around Europe on "$5 a Day." During this time we had a tape recorder and one cassette tape — "Tapestry" by Carole King — that we listened to every day. One of the songs, it turns out, carried a meaning for the profession we chose when we returned home. In one song Carole King observed...

We are all in this together

And maybe we'll see that one day

When we conquer our fear together

When we finally find a way.

One of our supreme frustrations over these 38 years has been to observe our field's inability to see that we are all in this together. Instead of working together to promote policies and programs that meet the

needs of all children and families, early childhood professionals too often worry more about the impact on the programs in their particular silo. Advocates for Head Start, family child care, for profit child care, community nonprofits, church-affiliated child care, and Pre-K in the public schools have tended to look out for what serves their community rather than the overall early childhood universe. The result is a mishmash of programs and policies that, in concert, do not add up to a coherent national approach to serving America's children and families.

The good news is that now there are some initiatives that point toward an increased interest in 'working together.' The Head Start community, thanks to the efforts of Linda Smith and the National Head Start Association, has been reaching out to operate programs in cooperation with community-based non profit and for profit programs. In addition, the Early Care and Education Consortium has made great progress in uniting many segments of the non profit and for profit provider communities in advocating for universally meaningful policies and programs at state and national levels.

Nothing Replaces the Value of Grit

One of the more memorable moments of the 1984 Summer Olympics in Los Angeles was the entry of Swiss marathoner Gabriel Andersen-Schiess into the Los Angeles Coliseum. The crowd gasped in horror as she staggered onto the track, her torso twisted, her left arm limp, her right leg mostly seized. She waved away medical personnel who rushed to help her, knowing that if they touched her, she would be disqualified. The Los Angeles Coliseum crowd applauded and cheered as she limped around the track in the race's final 400 meters, occasionally stopping and holding her head. At the completion of this final lap, she collapsed at the finish line and was rushed off by medics.

When Anderson-Schiess entered the stadium, she was totally spent. What kept her going was her absolute unswerving determination to finish the first-ever Women's Olympic Marathon. It was a dramatic demonstration of the importance of grit.

Now, center directors do not perform in front of tens of thousands of cheering fans, but the challenges they face often require as much sheer grit. A director can have great expertise in finance, marketing, and supervision — and an ebullient, charismatic personality — but all this talent is for naught if she can't hang in there when crises arise. Directors who cave in to all the pressures end up overseeing programs that descend into mediocrity or worse, or they walk away from the profession. Directors who are resilient enough to struggle through immense challenges and come out on the other side, standing proud and tall, make a huge contribution to the lives of children, families, and staff.

A Final Word

Most importantly, we've learned that early childhood professionals in programs of all configurations and organizational structures around the globe are determined, mission-driven, creative, great-hearted, visionary people. It continues to be our joy meeting and working with leaders who have the ability to craft inspiring and effective environments for adults and children in the face of enormous challenges.

References

McCormack, M. (1986). *What they don't teach you at Harvard Business School.* New York: Bantam.

Montagu, A. (1995, November/December). "Friendship — Loving: What Early Childhood Education is All About." *Exchange, 106,* 42-43.

Bonnie Neugebauer

Bonnie Neugebauer is Editor of *Exchange Magazine* and a co-founder of the World Forum Foundation.

Roger Neugebauer

Roger Neugebauer is publisher of *Exchange Magazine* and a co-founder of the World Forum Foundation.

the *Art of*
LEADERSHIP
LEADING
EARLY CHILDHOOD ORGANIZATIONS

2 CHAPTER 2
Supervising Staff

12 Reasons People Love to Work for You *by Roger Neugebauer* 46

Who Made Me Boss? *by Gigi Schweikert* 51

Self-Motivation: Motivation at Its Best *by Roger Neugebauer* 54

What Do Teachers Need Most from Their Directors? *by Margie Carter* 60

The Paradoxes of Leadership *by Bonnie Neugebauer and Roger Neugebauer* 65

You Say Staff Deserve Respect? Energize Your Words with Action! *by Karen Stephens* 69

Becoming an Authentic Communicator *by Johnna Darragh Ernst* 73

Building and Rebuilding Your Credibility *by Roger Neugebauer* 77

If Your Boss is the Problem, What Choices Do You Have? *by Holly Elissa Bruno* 81

12 Reasons People Love to Work for You

by Roger Neugebauer

The well director doesn't work to make people love her, but makes people love to work for her.

I proposed this maxim in an article, "The Well Director," in the March 1987 issue of *Exchange*. Since then a number of people (two) have said, "Well, that sounds just peachy; but how do you make people love to work for you in real life?"

So I've been keeping my eye on the directors of centers where teacher turnover is low, trying to figure out what they are doing right. Based on these observations, here are 12 practices you can implement to motivate people to stay: 12 reasons people will love to work for you.

1. You believe in people from day one.

With the shrinking supply of qualified teachers, there is a tendency to be pessimistic about the potential of the people we hire. This pessimism can result in a self-fulfilling prophecy: we don't expect high performance, so we don't make an effort to encourage high performance; and, in the end, we don't see high performance.

You can't manipulate people like puppets. They alone have the power to decide whether they will work hard. However, your attitude about a person can have a significant dampening or buoying impact on their self-confidence. When you believe a person has the potential to succeed, and when you believe that a person has a desire to succeed, your support can make a difference.

2. You build on people's strengths.

You will never find the perfect teacher, cook, bookkeeper, or bus driver (or spouse, for that matter). All of us have our shortcomings. However, we don't hire people because of their weaknesses. We hire them because we see some talent, some experience, or some trait that is a strength that we need.

To help new employees succeed on the job, you need to focus on the reasons you hired them. Time devoted to building on people's strengths is time well invested. Time spent in trying to fix people's weaknesses is, more often than not, time wasted.

There always will be occasions when you must affirmatively deal with poor performance, which is directly affecting the quality of your program:

conflict, absenteeism, inappropriate discipline, and so on. However, focusing all your energy on people's shortcomings results mostly in frustration, anger, and alienation (anyone with teenagers can relate to this).

One director I visited likes to get things off on the right foot by finding something a new employee will succeed in their first day. She assigns him or her some specific activity or task that employs a skill or training that the new employee possesses already.

Betty Jones from Pacific Oaks suggests that the early training teachers receive should build on the skills people bring to the job, even though these may not be the most important things they need to know to do their job. If you encourage new employees to improve on an area of strength, they will be less threatened because they are on turf that is comfortable and familiar to them. Then, as they feel rewarded by their improvement in a 'safe' area, you can gradually nudge them to grow in areas where they may feel less secure.

3. You provide people with feedback.

One of the most frequent complaints I hear from teachers is that they do not receive feedback on their efforts. They do not know if the director thinks they are doing a good job overall, or if the director even cares about what they are doing.

According to management guru Peter Drucker, what employees most need to improve their performance is an abundance of objective, timely feedback on the results of their performance. In well-functioning centers, the director places a high priority on encouraging staff to provide feedback to each other, in training staff on how to give feedback, and in providing time and tools for all types of feedback systems.

4. You view people's welfare as a high priority.

When it comes to worker compensation, we all sing the same tune. We all lament the low wages and benefits our teachers receive. But passionate speeches don't pay the rent.

There are no easy solutions to the compensation dilemma. No knight in shining armor is going to charge in and save the day in the foreseeable future — not the federal government, not employers, and not Bill Gates.

The solution will primarily come from tough choices and hard compromises, made one center at a time. A director who is truly committed to making progress on the compensation issue will be educating parents and raising fees, and will be actively exploring creative solutions to improving benefits.

Over the past four decades, my wife Bonnie and I have visited hundreds of early childhood programs all around the world. And we commonly observe that when there are many programs struggling under the same constraints, serving the same markets, there are always one or two programs that, through creativity and hard work, manage to pay their teachers 10% to 20% higher than all the other programs.

Teachers lose faith in a director who decries low wages, but refuses to raise fees for fear of upsetting parents. The bottom line is that teachers' commitment will be impacted by whether or not they perceive that you truly do place a high priority on their welfare and are seen doing something about it.

5. You build team spirit.

Clare Cherry, in addition to all her writing and speaking, actually directed a child care center in San Bernardino, California. In interviewing prospective teachers, she informed them that if they were to work at her center, they would be required to accept responsibility for helping all the teachers improve.

Teachers at Clare's center were expected to share ideas, to give each other feedback, to solve problems together, and to provide each other support. She viewed teamwork as an essential ingredient of an excellent program. And for team spirit to flower, it requires such commitment from the top to make it happen.

You need to be continually exploring ways to encourage cooperative efforts, whether it means rotating the chairperson at staff meetings, regularly conducting brainstorming sessions to attack center problems, or taking the entire staff on a retreat. Team building needs to be a conscious activity promoted by the director, attended to by the director, and rewarded by the director.

6. You inspire commitment.

One of the responsibilities of the leader in any organization is to serve as the keeper of the faith. You need to have a vision for your organization that gives meaning to your work and inspires you to act.

If you have such a vision, this will not only inspire you, but it should inspire everyone who works in the organization. Directors I have observed who are committed to a vision exude intensity and excitement, which energizes everyone in their centers.

When people are committed to the goals of an organization, they will work hard to ensure that these goals are achieved. This is much more powerful than trying to build people's commitment to you as an individual.

7. You set high standards.

In the very best centers I visit, the directors have an unflagging commitment to high performance. Even when crises seem to be breaking out all over, these

directors do not allow these frustrations to serve as an excuse for letting up on quality.

Achieving high standards in a child care center is indeed a very imposing challenge. Pressure to maintain these standards can understandably put a heavy burden on all staff. However, these frustrations are far outweighed by the feeling of pride that comes from working in a first class organization.

8. You remove obstacles to people's success.

The most effective directors I see do not view themselves as making things happen by sitting atop the chain of command issuing orders and making inspirational speeches. Rather, they view themselves as servants to the team

These directors see their job as helping teachers succeed by getting them the resources they need to grow and perform. They take seriously the responsibility of removing obstacles that get in the way of people doing their jobs, whether it be replacing equipment that's worn out or reorganizing a staffing structure that doesn't work.

9. You encourage people to take risks.

We all view ourselves as open, supportive, and encouraging. But sometimes our intentions are belied by our actions.

We may encourage staff to be creative, yet convey through body language a sense of disapproval when they try a new activity and it fails. We may ask people for their solutions to a center problem, but find fault with or ignore any suggestions they make.

If you expect your people to act creatively, you have to send a strong message that you support them. You must praise people for taking risks. You need to thank people for having the courage to disagree with you. You must provide a rich environment of books, materials, trips, and workshops to keep people thinking and growing. And, most importantly, you should demonstrate that you are willing to take risks yourself.

10. You make working fun.

One of the most consistent features of centers where teachers love to work is a relaxed, happy atmosphere. Child care is hard work with serious implications. But no one can thrive without laughter or joy.

When I visit a center, an instant barometer of the quality of the program is if I hear laughter — laughter in the classrooms, laughter in the teachers' lounge, laughter in the director's office. Bonnie and I visited a child care program in an impoverished township outside of Johannesburg, South Africa, where 20 young children were crowded into a room with a dirt floor and no windows and no fancy colorful toys. But in the dancing and singing of those children (and their teachers), we saw great joy.

Having fun does not mean bringing clowns into the classrooms or comedians into staff meetings. It means appreciating, allowing, and encouraging a playful spirit in children and adults.

11. You cultivate professional pride.

A disquieting aspect of the media attention child care often receives has been the 'crisis' mode of this coverage. Documentary after documentary, and article after article, decries how horrible child care conditions are in this country (especially when compared, over and over again, with the Swedish child care system).

This coverage may serve a purpose in focusing attention on the need for additional resources to assist low-income families and to improve working conditions. However, it has also tended to give a negative image of our profession and to disparage the valiant efforts of those working in centers and family child care homes.

The director on the cover of the November 1990 issue of *Exchange*, Isabella Graham, opened the first child care center in the nation more than 155 years ago. In that issue we included a list of the 50 oldest centers in the nation, which included 21 centers that have been in operation over 100 years.

Child care is not a recent fad or new profession struggling to get its act together. We have a long, proud tradition of caring. We make it possible for our nation's economy to function. We are providing a nurturing, stimulating start in life for millions of children. You need to enable staff to take pride in being a part of the early childhood profession.

12. You help people see results.

Lilian Katz, in an article, "On Teaching," in the February 1990 issue of *Exchange* noted that every semester there will be two or three of her students who reveal that a single teacher, by showing concern or encouragement, saved their psychological lives. Katz concludes: "Just think how many children that adds up to over a career of teaching… it could be more than 100 people. That's a lot of lives to make a real difference to."

As a director, the most effective way you can get teachers hooked on continuing in your center is to help them see the real impact they are having on the lives of children. You can do this by training teachers to be better observers so they can see the children progress, by encouraging teachers to give each other feedback on the changes they observe, and, foremost, by encouraging parents to share their joy over the progress their children are making.

Knowing that you were responsible for helping a shy child come out of his shell or an overly aggressive child calm down is a type of reward that very few professions can offer.

William Franklin, speaking at an *Exchange* conference in New Orleans, quoted the remarks made by Pericles to his troops, noting that he could just as well have been addressing early childhood professionals:

"What you leave behind is not what is engraved in stone monuments, but what is woven into the lives of others."

There are many great reasons for working in early childhood, not the least of which is the real difference we can make in the lives of the children and families we serve. Helping teachers see their great impact will inspire them to survive and thrive in your program.

Roger Neugebauer

Roger Neugebauer is publisher of *Exchange Magazine* and a co-founder of the World Forum Foundation.

Who Made Me Boss?

by Gigi Schweikert

You know those early childhood teachers who are absolutely amazing? The ones who can manage 20 children inside on a rainy day all by themselves, make dough out of air, construct an entire addition to their center using only toilet paper rolls and duct tape, create a complete curriculum of science, math, social studies, and more based on one pumpkin seed? And of course, those amazing teachers can figure out 'coverage' even if six teachers are sick, two can't lift anything over ten pounds, and one teacher is leaving early. Those amazing teachers are the ones I call the 'master teachers.'

Becoming a Supervisor

You know what happens to most master teachers? They are asked to be supervisors so they can teach other staff members how to do all the great things they do. Unfortunately, most master teachers do what they do naturally, and working well with children doesn't always translate into working well with adults.

Whether you're a director, program coordinator, or lead teacher, supervising other adults is probably the hardest part of your job. You're good! That's how you got where you are, but doing everything by yourself and complaining about it won't make you a good supervisor.

So what does makes a good leader? Everyone's style is different, but in my experience a boss "tells you what to do," a manager "motivates you to do stuff," and a leader "inspires you to be the best you can be." Being a good supervisor requires you to be all three at times, but most importantly, and all the time, you need to be a leader.

Eight Supervision Tips

Listed are some ideas to help you become a better supervisor and inspire those around you:

1. Admit You're the Supervisor

Admitting to yourself that you're the supervisor is not a bad thing. In the corporate world success is measured by title, salary, and the number of people under you. Somehow, in the child care field, we're not always proud of being in charge. Working directly with children seems the most worthy responsibility in our industry. But good supervisors are not only necessary, they're helpful. There must have been a person, a supervisor, who inspired you to continue in the early childhood field. Think of the positive skills of that supervisor. What can you use in your own leadership? Concentrate on being respected rather than being liked. Try to make the right decisions, not popular decisions.

2. Make Your Expectations Clear

The majority of employees want to do a good job. They want to please you and others. Suppose you hired me as a substitute? Think I'd do a good job? I'd try to apply my skills, but in spite of my experience I couldn't do my best for you unless you told me what you need. I don't know that Mark's and Tasha's mats don't go side-by-side, where to get the glue, or how lunch is set up. Supervisors have to tell their employees what they want them to do, and supervisors need to be specific. Employees feel awkward if they don't know or understand their responsibilities. When a job isn't done well, first question whether you communicated your expectations clearly.

3. Create a Culture that Encourages New Ideas and Allows for Mistakes

Developing clear expectations for your employees doesn't mean there aren't lots of opportunities for employees to be creative and involved. Develop a supportive work environment that encourages new ideas and allows for mistakes. Never compromise the safety of children. Leaving children unattended or falling asleep at naptime are not mistakes; they're irresponsible. But encouraging another staff member to coordinate Grandparent's Day, plan the daily curriculum, or even organize and carry out circle time are opportunities to let teachers use and improve their skills. There's more than one way to make Jell-O®. So what if it doesn't gel. There's a science lesson in there somewhere. Encourage individual thinking. Make it easy for employees to give ideas through meetings, one-on-one conversations, and written suggestions. Once new ideas are in-hand, follow through on their ideas so employees know that you value their contributions.

4. Don't Get in the Way of Success

Can you let the process and results of a job be different from the way you would do it? Try to avoid the "Do it my Way" approach to supervision. Employees whose work is constantly criticized or redone because there is only one way to get things done eventually stop trying. And guess what? You're on your own to do it your way.

Everyone has skills and talents. Emphasize the skill or goal rather than the process or method. Allow freedom of expression. Don't stand in the way of teachers doing their job. Delegate a job and stand back. You'll be surprised and your employees will feel empowered, trusted, and proud! Build on success. There's more than one way to get things done.

5. Communicate Honestly

I'm the kind of person who definitely wants to be told if I come out of the bathroom with toilet paper stuck on my shoe. Ever check out your teeth in the mirror only to see a big hunk of broccoli or something, and wonder how long it was there and why no one told you? It's the same with supervision. Keeping employees adequately informed and telling employees about hunks of broccoli in their performance are only fair. Be honest. Let people know where they stand.

You're not a *meanie* if you accurately provide your employees with feedback on their work. On the contrary, good supervisors describe to employees how they are doing and how they can improve. Surprise! We can all improve. As Jim Greenman said, "Good enough, never is." Tell employees right away about any changes that will affect them and about things that won't affect them, so they won't worry. In the absence of information, people speculate and gossip. I call that 'playground chatter.'

6. Follow Through

I think supervisors with the greatest credibility are not only honest, but follow through on what they promise. Child care is a busy world and no matter how well your "To-Do List" is scripted, the events of the day will rewrite your list and priorities. State licensing always shows up on the day the oven breaks and you're stuck making 200 peanut butter and jelly sandwiches, a gerbil is on the loose somewhere in the building, and your entire afternoon staff is going to be 'a little late.' So how do you follow through? Develop clear, realistic expectations of yourself. Stick to policy, but be open to policy change. Don't waiver on consequences when an employee neglects responsibility. If you request curriculum plans to be turned in every Thursday, then stick to it. And if you promised to make comments and return the plans, then do it.

Sometimes following through after a very busy day is just a call to say, "I promised to get back to you this afternoon about your concern. I will have to meet with you tomorrow." If you find you're failing to follow through often, reexamine your expectations and those put upon you by staff. It's okay to say to an employee, "I know this project is important to you and I can discuss it next week." You don't have to make every decision when someone grabs you in the hall.

7. Stay Connected

Develop ways to stay in touch with your employees, especially if you work side by side in the classroom. Good supervisors need adult time away from the children to reflect and talk. Weekly head teacher or classroom meetings, quarterly goals, annual performance appraisals, and frequent one-on-ones may seem like too much time to invest. Actually, defined opportunities for supervisor and employees to meet cut down on, "May I talk to you for a minute?" and lines at your door. Supervisors and employees learn to hold their issues and ideas for meeting time instead of chatting in front of the children.

As a supervisor, you want to maintain an, "*I'm approachable, I'm available, open door policy,*" but important issues and policy decisions require Kascheduled time on the calendar. Supervisors are kind of like banks; your ATM is always open for a quick withdrawal or balance update, but refinancing requires employees to come in and sit down. Stay connected.

8. Set the Tone

As a leader, your attitude sets the tone of the center or classroom. Are you hurried and frantic? Are you determined to get things accomplished, but are relaxed? Which style would better motivate you? When something goes wrong, help employees feel a problem is their problem, too. Don't look for someone to blame. Build your team by asking employees for their advice and help. Leaders don't know all the answers, but they do surround themselves with people who can help them figure it out.

Give authority with responsibility. It inspires staff. When the job gets heated, be the thermostat not the thermometer. Establish a calm, supportive environment where adults and children feel comfortable and at home. No one likes to work at 110%. But as a leader you can inspire those around you to be at 110%.

Gigi Schweikert

Gigi Schweikert is the working mother of four children and author of 18 books on parenting and early childhood education, including the best-selling *Winning Ways series* with Redleaf Press. With 25 years' experience, Gigi's practical ideas and realistic perspective on child care will have you laughing and learning. Gigi's an international keynote speaker, recently in Malaysia and New Zealand, and she'd love to come to your program, no matter where you are. She's on the advisory board of KidReports and believes technology can keep us connected.

Self-Motivation

Motivation at Its Best

by Roger Neugebauer

The director of Mother Goose Child Care Center was concerned. Incidents of lateness and absenteeism among her teachers were increasing. The teachers had stopped planning activities in advance and showed little enthusiasm in working with the children. They also complained continually about everything from inadequate equipment to low wages.

She decided that what was needed to improve staff performance was to tighten discipline. She required teachers to submit daily lesson plans for her approval. She had them sign in and out and deducted pay for lateness and unexcused absences. She kept a closer watch on the classrooms and reprimanded teachers who were sloughing off.

The results were mixed. Lateness and absenteeism declined, and lesson plans were being developed; but teachers' attitudes became even worse. They complained more and acted as if working in the classroom were a drudgery.

Next the director tried the opposite approach. She sought to cheer the staff up by granting them wage increases, setting up a comfortable teachers' lounge, and holding occasional staff parties.

Once again she was disappointed. Although the staff acted happier and complained less, they still exhibited little enthusiasm in their work with the children.

The Jackass Fallacy

One reason the director's remedies failed is that she was operating from overly simplistic notions about what motivates people to work hard. She acted as if the teachers were naturally lazy and irresponsible, as if they could only be made to work hard through fear of punishment or promise of rewards. This carrot-and-stick approach may work perfectly well in motivating a jackass, but it is wholly inappropriate in motivating people. As Harry Levinson, creator of the *Jackass Fallacy* analogy, explains:

"As long as anyone in a leadership role operates with such a reward-punishment attitude toward motivation, he is implicitly assuming that he has control over others and that they are in a jackass position with respect to him. This attitude is inevitably one of condescending contempt whose most blatant mask is paternalism. The result is a continuing battle between those who seek to wield power and those who are subject to it."

What Does Motivate Teachers?

This author interviewed 64 child care teachers about what satisfies them and what frustrates them in their work. In reviewing the major sources of satisfaction (see summary on next page), it can be seen that they relate directly to the *content* of the teachers' work. These factors — observing progress in children, relationships with children — result directly from the way teachers perform their work. On the other hand, the major sources of frustration — rate of pay, supervision, personnel policies — relate to the *environment* in which the work is performed.

Based on similar findings in studies in a wide variety of professions (see Herzberg), organizational psychologists have reached a number of conclusions on what can be done to motivate workers. When the environmental factors are not adequately provided for (i.e., when pay is low or the environment is oppressive), workers will become frustrated. However, when these factors are adequately provided for, this will usually have no important positive effect — these factors do nothing to elevate an individual's desire to do his job well. The content-related factors, commonly referred to as motivators, on the other hand, can stimulate workers to perform well. They provide a genuine sense of satisfaction.

A director seeking to bolster the sagging morale of her teachers, therefore, will have only limited success if she focuses solely on the environmental factors — increasing pay, improving physical arrangements, making supervision less rigid. If the teachers' lounge is renovated, teachers may become less frustrated, but they won't necessarily work harder on the

job because of this change. To truly motivate the teachers, a director needs to focus her attention on restructuring the teachers' jobs so that they can derive more satisfaction directly from their work.

Examining Motivators More Closely

But how does one go about restructuring a teacher's job to take advantage of these motivating factors? Taking a cue from organizational psychologists, a director should strive to meet the following criteria in restructuring a job (Hackman):

1. **Meaningfulness.** A teacher must feel her work is important, valuable, and worthwhile. If a teacher believes her work is unimportant, it won't really matter to her whether or not she does it well. If she believes her teaching does have a significant impact on children's lives, she will work hard to see that the impact is a positive one.

2. **Responsibility.** A teacher must feel personally responsible and accountable for the results of the work he performs. If a teacher is simply carrying out the plans and instructions of a supervisor, he will derive little personal satisfaction when things go well. If he has complete control over the planning and implementation of daily activities in his room, he will know that when children are thriving it is due to his efforts.

3. **Knowledge of results.** A teacher must receive regular feedback on the results of her efforts. If a teacher exerts a major effort on an activity but receives no indication as to whether or not it was successful, she will gain no satisfaction. A teacher can only derive satisfaction from the positive results she knows about.

The remainder of this article will be devoted to describing specific examples of how to apply these criteria.

Clarifying Goals

Before teachers can be satisfied with the results of their efforts, they must be clear as to what results were expected in the first place. The center must have goals which teachers can use as yardsticks to evaluate their accomplishments. To be effective, a center's goals must:

1. Be compatible with the personal goals of teachers. Teachers will work hardest to accomplish organizational goals that are most similar to their own goals. Some centers achieve a close fit between organizational and personal goals by involving the teachers in developing the goals at the beginning of the year. Other organizations accomplish this by holding planning conferences between the director and individual staff members. In these conferences the employee outlines her personal interest and career goals. The two then develop ways in which the individual can work toward the accomplishment of her goals and the organization's goals at the same time (McGregor). For example, if one of a teacher's goals is to develop her creative movement skills and one of the center's goals is to stimulate children's imaginations, the teacher might be assigned to develop and use movement activities that challenge children's imaginations.

2. Provide a moderate challenge to teachers. Experiments have shown that most workers respond best to goals, which are moderately difficult to achieve (Gellerman). The goal must not be so ambitious that it cannot possibly be achieved, nor so easy that it can be accomplished with little effort. Such moderately challenging goals should be established for the program as a whole (for example, to double the amount of cooperative play among the children) as well as for individual children (i.e., to help David control his temper).

Encouraging Self-control

A key to outgrowing a jackass style of management is shifting control over teachers' performances from the director to the teachers themselves. Ideally, a teacher and a director could agree upon a set of goals for a classroom at the beginning of the year. The teacher would then be fully responsible for planning and implementing daily activities to achieve these goals. At the end of a set time period (the less experienced the staff, the more modest the goals and the shorter the time period) the teacher would be held accountable for having accomplished the goals. The teacher would work hard, not because he was being closely watched by the director, but because he was personally committed to achieving the goals.

Centers have developed many ways of supporting teachers in controlling their own performance. One center has the teachers write and periodically revise their job descriptions and the rules for various classroom areas. Another provides teachers with sufficient petty cash so they won't have to keep running to the director to request money to buy routine supplies and equipment. A third has teachers bring problems with children before their peers so that teachers can learn to solve their own problems.

Major Sources of Satisfaction and Frustration

In a survey of 64 teachers in 24 New England child care programs, the following were identified as their major sources of satisfaction and frustration in their work. (They are listed in order of frequency.)

Sources of Satisfaction

1. Observing progress in children
2. Relationships with children
3. Challenge of the work
4. Pride in performing a service
5. Relationships with parents
6. Recognition shown by staff

Sources of Frustration

1. Rate of pay
2. Prospects for advancement
3. Physical work environment

4. Style of supervision
5. Number of hours worked
6. Inflexible personnel policies

Not all teachers will be willing or able to function so independently. Some will always feel more comfortable having someone else take the lead and issue directions. Other teachers may be ready to accept responsibility, but not for a full classroom. These teachers could have their self-control supported by being assigned full responsibility for a small number of children, for a certain activity area, or for performing a specific function (such as offering support and encouragement to children).

Providing Feedback

When teachers were asked what satisfies them, they happily cited incidents such as: "When children beam after finally accomplishing a task"; "Seeing examples of children's cooperative play steadily increase"; or "When a parent comments on how a child's behavior is dramatically improving at home thanks to the school."

Given the high motivational impact of incidents such as these, a director should give high priority to seeing to it that they happen as often as possible. To get an idea of how a director might do this, the hundreds of motivating incidents supplied by teachers were analyzed. The majority of these incidents were found to fall into three primary categories, which are listed below. With each category, ideas are listed that a director can use to encourage that type of motivation.

1. Immediate reactions of children to an activity or to accomplishing a task.

■ Help teachers develop their skills in observing children's subtle signs of change or satisfaction.

■ Ask teachers to list incidents of children's reactions and changes (pro and con) on a single day or week. This will force them to be alert for such feedback that they may otherwise be too preoccupied to notice.

■ Periodically ask parents for incidents of children's progress or follow through on school activities. Pass these on to the children's teachers.

■ Recruit volunteers to teach so that teachers can occasionally step back and observe what's going on in the classroom.

■ Provide feedback to teachers focusing on effects of teaching on children rather than on the teachers' methods or styles.

■ Set aside a time on Fridays when teachers can pause to reflect on what went wrong and what went right during the week. Devote occasional staff meetings to having teachers share their good experiences from the week.

2. Warm relationships established with the children and their parents.

■ Provide times and places where teachers can have relaxed, intimate conversations with individual children.

■ Make teachers responsible for a small number of children, so they can get to know each other better.

■ Before the school year begins, have teachers visit children's homes to establish rapport with the families.

■ Encourage families to keep in touch with the center after their children graduate.

■ Assign each teacher responsibility for maintaining regular communications with specific parents.

■ Bring in volunteers at the end or beginning of the day so that teachers can have informal, uninterrupted conversations with parents.

3. Indications of the long-range progress of children.

■ Make teachers responsible for long periods of time for complete units of work. If teachers' responsibilities are continuously shifting from one group of children to another, or from one curriculum area to another, they will never be able to attribute any long-term changes in children primarily to their own efforts.

■ Keep diaries of children's behavior so that changes in children can be tracked.

■ Videotape classroom activities periodically and compare children's behavior as the year progresses.

■ At regular intervals tabulate the number of incidents of specific behaviors that occur in a set time period to determine if there are any changes in these behaviors.

■ Conduct tests on the developmental levels of children throughout the year.

■ In regular parent conferences, with teachers present, ask parents to discuss changes they have noted in their children's behavior.

Promoting Staff Development

One of the most important ways a director can help motivate teachers is to provide them with opportunities to improve their skills. The more skilled teachers are, the more likely they are to experience, and be rewarded by, incidents of success. The director should help teachers identify their specific training needs and secure appropriate training resources. These resources may be in the form of reading material, in-house staff training sessions, or outside workshops and courses.

Encouraging Broader Involvement

Most teachers will tend to feel better about themselves, as well as more excited about their work, if they are involved in their profession outside the classroom. If teachers are involved in the overall management of their center or in children's advocacy efforts in the community, they will get a stronger sense of their efforts being an integral part of a vital profession.

At the center level, teachers' involvement can be broadened by keeping them continually informed on the status of the organization as a whole, by assigning them limited administrative responsibilities, as well as by involving them, wherever feasible, in major center decisionmaking.

Centers have also experienced positive results from encouraging their teachers to become involved in professional activities outside the center. Such activities might include participating in advocacy coalitions, working for professional organizations (such as NAEYC chapters), or promoting various child care alternatives in the community. Active teacher involvement in these areas will also relieve some pressure on the director to be the agency's representative on every committee and function.

Motivation — A Final Perspective

The message of this article is that teachers are their own best source of motivation. If a teacher's work is properly structured, she will be motivated by the results of her own labors, not by external rewards and punishments manipulated by someone else. The director's prime concern should, therefore, be with helping the teacher achieve control over and feedback from her work.

This is not to say, however, that the director need not be concerned with environmental factors such as wages, personnel policies, and physical environment. Highly motivated teachers will be very tolerant of unavoidable inadequacies in these areas. However, if conditions deteriorate markedly, especially if this appears to be due to the indifference of management, teachers' motivation will rapidly be cancelled out by their growing frustration. Therefore, in motivating teachers by concentrating attention on job content, the director should not ignore the teachers' basic needs.

References and Resources

Gellerman, S. W. (1963). *Motivation and productivity*. New York: American Management Association.

Hackman, J. R., & Suttle, J. L (1977). *Improving life at work.* Santa Monica, CA: Goodyear Publishing Company.

Herzberg, F. (January-February 1968). "One More Time: How Do You Motivate Employees?" *Harvard Business Review.*

Levinson, H. (January-February 1973). "Asinine Attitudes Toward Motivation." *Harvard Business Review.*

McGregor, D. (1960). *The human side of enterprise.* New York: McGraw-Hill Book Company.

Neugebauer, R. "Organizational Analysis of Day Care." ERIC Document Reproduction Service PO Box 190, Arlington, VA 22210.

Roger Neugebauer

Roger Neugebauer is publisher of *Exchange Magazine* and a co-founder of the World Forum Foundation.

What Do Teachers Need Most from Their Directors?

by Margie Carter

"Perceptions are powerful regulators of behavior that can influence teachers' level of commitment to a center. In fact, people's perceptions of events may be more important than reality because individuals act according to their interpretation of events."

Paula Jorde Bloom, *Circle of Influence*
(New Horizons, 2000)

Over the last eight months, I've been doing an informal research project. Nothing scientific. No statistical analysis. Just keeping my ears finely tuned and asking a few focused questions as I work with child care teachers at their program sites and in seminars at conferences. There is now an established process called 'participatory research,' but I can't claim to have been even that systematic in my inquiry. Mostly, I've just been trying to carefully listen for what management styles, dispositions, and skills engender confidence and respect from staff toward their director. Are there particular philosophies, policies, decision-making and communication systems that influence teachers to stay at their workplace longer, despite inadequate salaries and benefits?

What I've consistently heard from teachers reflects the research behind several important publications in our field:

■ Paula Jorde Bloom's two books, *A Great Place to Work: Improving Conditions for Staff in Young Children's Programs* and *Circle of Influence: Implementing Shared Decision Making and Participative Management*

■ The Center for the Child Care Workforce (CCW) publication, *Creating Better Child Care Jobs: Model Work Standards for Teaching Staff in Center-based Child Care*

Bloom discusses her research on how the interplay between people and the environment, and between work attitudes and group dynamics, supports the professionalism of an organization. In discussing the concept of organizational climate, she says: "Although it is not clear whether climate or satisfaction comes first, job satisfaction seems to be higher in schools with relatively open climates. These climates are characterized by a sense of belonging, many opportunities to interact, autonomy, and upward influence." (1997)

More recently, through the efforts of the Center for the Child Care Workforce, early childhood program staff themselves have been developing an assessment tool, the *Model Work Standards*, which highlights the components of work environments that are linked to quality for children in our programs. This tool is a welcome addition to our field and substantiates Bloom's point:

"One valuable insight gained during an assessment of employee attitudes about their work environment is the sharper understanding of where perceptions differ between administrators and employees. One of the more common findings, for example, is that directors often believe they give far more feedback to their staff than their teachers perceive they get. Another common difference is found in the directors' and staff's perceptions regarding staff involvement in decisions about practices to be followed in the center... directors typically rate the climate more favorably than do teachers." (1997)

The impetus for my own investigation into what teachers want from their directors stems from continually hearing examples of differing perceptions between directors and staff in their rating of the work environment. It strikes me that because directors work so hard and under such stress, they are sometimes reluctant to welcome staff perspectives on what needs changing if there aren't resources or time to commit to an issue. However, I've discovered that when directors welcome feedback on how the work environment feels, they unlock the potential for creative problem solving. A tool such as the *Model Work Standards* helps directors clearly see where their program should be headed. As with accreditation criteria, it can serve as a weather gauge for the organizational climate and a concrete reference point for budgeting and/or grant writing.

In *A Great Place to Work*, Paula Jorde Bloom is instructive about the dimensions of an organizational climate that need tending to in our early childhood programs. She is also quite persuasive in *Circle of Influence*, detailing the value of shared decision making and participative management. What she says in these two publications outlining her research

is what I have been hearing in my informal, yet careful listening work with teachers.

As I ask, "What do teachers need most from their directors," either as a direct question to them or as I focus my listening and watching, I consistently hear a call for tending to the physical, social, and emotional environment of the program. These are my categories for their ideas, different from but interrelated to the research message from Bloom and the Center for the Child Care Workforce.

Offer Genuine Respect and Trust

The words 'trust' and 'respect' easily roll off our tongues, and our heads nod when we hear them, but what do these words look like in action? Teachers say they usually feel respected when someone really listens to them, trying to understand and be responsive, rather than just placating. Some talk about 'being trusted to succeed,' even if they falter or 'goof up.' But they are quick to add that respect and trust means being given the time, support, and tools they need, not leaving them alone to sink or swim but neither hovering nor micro-managing. "When I'm really listened to and taken seriously, I feel validated and respected." Others use the word 'empowered' along with trust and respect. One teacher commented: "Empowerment can be a bogus word. No one can give you your power, but they can disempower you, taking away your self-trust and respect. When your director trusts you, you are motivated to use your power to learn and get it right."

Some teachers claim that directors only show trust and respect to staff members who agree with them. This clearly undermines what Bloom refers to as 'collegiality' in naming ten important dimensions in an organizational climate. Posting a sign or announcing "We will all respect each other here" irritates some teachers. You can't mandate trust and respect. These feelings have to be developed over time with accumulated experiences to confirm or counter our initial impressions.

Trust comes more quickly when we work from both our heads and our hearts. As we become clear about our values and ideas, and learn to communicate them with a blend of honesty and empathy, respect for different points of view can grow. We don't have to become best friends to trust each other, but we do have to have mutual respect and be able to count on each other if genuine trust is to grow and thrive.

Work With a Vision

It's striking to hear teachers describe the contrast between directors who work with a vision and those who settle for how things are. The word 'vision' isn't always used, but they excitedly describe how their director really inspired them to work at the center, how "she's usually got a twinkle in her eye," is always "showing us pictures or little quotes to expand our thinking," or "keeps her eye on the prize even when our budget comes up short." Perhaps some of this is related to the dimension Bloom calls 'innovation' or 'goal consensus.' Teachers can sense when directors are moving their program forward toward a bigger dream, even as they are thwarted by the crisis of the week. The climate is quite different than one limited to following the rules and regulations or resigning the program to the limitations of the moment.

Teachers acknowledge that directors with big dreams can sometimes overlook the trees for the forest. They can get caught up in grant writing, meetings in the community, or calls and visits to their legislators and neglect a child, parent, or teacher requiring immediate attention, film waiting to be developed, or a promised professional training opportunity. Most teachers don't just want to be kept informed of where the director is heading; they want a role in shaping a vision for the program. When they are offered this involvement, their energy and talents can be tapped and their commitment to the program grows. This is a very different experience for staff than merely delegating responsibility for some tasks the director can't get to. Teachers not only want to work with visionary directors, they want to dream and plan along with them.

Share the Decision-making Process

"I hate it when our director has made a decision and then goes through the motions of asking for our input. It's a waste of time and makes me resentful." CCW's *Model Work Standards* have several components that address this common sentiment from teachers. Their categories of communication, team building, and staff meetings, as well as decision making and problem solving, offer important descriptions of what teachers deem as necessary in a quality work environment. Bloom, in turn, has devoted a book in her *Director's Toolbox* series to the topic of implementing shared decision making and participative management. *Circle of Influence* outlines principles and values that support collaborative decision making and offers guidelines for determining decision-making processes and avoiding pitfalls. Bloom says:

"It is not enough to embrace the beliefs and values surrounding participation. Organizational structures and processes must be adapted so that staff and other stakeholders have the power and capacity to participate actively in decision-making ventures."

Teachers want clarity in the process for making decisions about things, which impact their ability to do their jobs well. Many want more than that and are eager to be mentored in understanding the big picture and learning consensus-building skills. They want their directors to offer strong leadership in getting all voices to the table. Teachers are intuitively clear about the difference between autocratic and democratic leadership, often mentioning the way their director succeeds or fails to facilitate the group dynamics so that everyone has power and input and teachers cultivate their own leadership skills.

Reject a Scarcity Mentality

Related to working with vision is the idea that teachers don't want their directors to just settle for how things are. They need to see and hear their directors pushing ahead with improvements in their compensation and working conditions.

A wonderful example of this can be found in an article by Carl Sussman, "Out of the Basement: Discovering the Value of Child Care Facilities." Sussman's specific focus is a story of a Head Start director with a vision to create an inspiring new building, but the lessons for directors are even broader — what I call rejecting a scarcity mentality. Sussman puts it this way: "To conserve energy for the educational tasks at hand, many teachers and administrators learn to live with modest expectations. They avoid disappointment by sacrificing their vision… [they] need to cultivate the cognitive dissonance of living with inadequate facilities while harboring an ambitious vision that could sustain a greatly enhanced program."

Teachers have many ways of describing the scarcity mentality they experience in their directors, be it excessive penny pinching, power holding as if there's only so much available, failure to network and connect with outside resources, or repeated responses to new ideas with a "They won't let us" or "No way! We can't afford it." They describe directors who inspire and sustain them with contrasting responses such as "Let's see how we could make that work" or "You're pushing me beyond what I know how to do, but I want to take up that challenge."

Tend to the Physical Environment

The typical early childhood program is situated in a less than ideal space with more limitations than we know what to do with. In his article, Sussman describes our situation this way: "Years of budget balancing and widespread acceptance of inadequate facilities has desensitized providers to their environment and created chronically low

expectations." In his article, he goes on to describe how the physical quality of a center can influence the way teachers interact with children and has the potential to reduce staff turnover rates. Indeed, one of the component areas of the *Model Work Standards* is the physical setting, where what teachers need for the children and themselves is delineated.

Most early childhood programs don't draw on the research from other professions about the impact of space, light, and color on behavior. We often furnish our programs with little attention to aesthetics or imagination. Across the country, many early childhood programs have begun to look alike, a mini replica of an early childhood catalog. Usually there are child-sized tables and chairs, primary colors, an abundance of plastic materials, commercial toys, and bulletin board displays. You have to search to find soft or natural elements, places where adults as well as children can feel cozy, alone, or with a friend. The smell of disinfectant often floats in the air. Have we forgotten how a cluttered or tattered environment quickly seeps into our psyche? Do we know how a sterile and antiseptic climate shapes our soul?

Caregivers, teachers, and children are spending the bulk of their waking hours living their lives together in our programs. The way we organize the space, create traffic and communication patterns, furnish and decorate all affect the experience people have in our buildings. When I listen for what teachers want from their directors, there is always something about improving the physical environment. In our book, *The Visionary Director*, Deb Curtis and I offer scores of ideas for creating an environment for adults that not only meets their needs, but parallels what we want them to be providing for children: softness; beauty; order; reflections of their interests, culture, and home life; things to discover and invent with; a place for personal belongings; and so forth. When directors give attention to the physical environment, it nourishes everyone involved and creates an on-going sense of possibilities.

Walk Your Talk

Again and again, teachers tell me there's nothing worse than a director who doesn't walk her talk. Promises without follow through, martyring oneself rather than modeling self-care, making excuses rather than making things happen are all behaviors that erode trust and respect. If you say you want more diversity in your program, then you must change the things that are keeping your program homogeneous. When you articulate a vision for your program, you must grow your way into it with how you set priorities and goals, create an environment and organizational culture, harness resources, and conduct human interactions. Listening to what teachers need from their directors can be a superficial endeavor or one that deepens understandings and broadens possibilities. It also contributes to a more stable, committed staff.

References and Resources

Bloom, P. J. (1997). *A great place to work: Improving conditions for staff in young children's programs* (Revised edition). Washington, DC: NAEYC.

Bloom, P. J. (2000). *Circle of influence: Implementing shared decision making and participative management.* New Horizons, PO Box 863, Lake Forest, IL 60045-0863, (847) 295-8131.

Carter, M., & Curtis, D. (1998). *The visionary director: A handbook for dreaming, organizing, & improvising in your center.* St Paul, MN: Redleaf Press.

The Center for the Child Care Workforce (1998). *Creating better child care jobs: Model work standards for teaching staff in center-based child care.* The Center for the Child Care Workforce, 733 15th Street NW, Suite 1037, Washington, DC 20005-2112, (202) 737-7700, fax: (202) 737-0370 (ccw@ccw.org).

Sussman, C. (1998). Out of the basement: Discovering the value of child care facilities. *Young Children, 1,* 15.

Margie Carter

Margie Carter is the co-founder of Harvest Resources Associates (www.ecetrainers.com) and the co-author of numerous books and early childhood videos. As she moves towards retirement years, her professional work is focused on highlighting and supporting the inspiring work of new leaders and uplifting the voices and leadership of teachers in the field.

The Paradoxes of Leadership

by Bonnie Neugebauer and Roger Neugebauer

In the past 20 years, we have had the opportunity to observe hundreds upon hundreds of leaders in action in child care centers. In addition, we have had 20 years to develop our leadership on the job as we struggled, sailed, failed, and succeeded in growing Exchange. *From all of these experiences, we have learned a few things about the paradoxes of leadership.*

Paradox #1
You need to enjoy your work, but you can't avoid the uglies.

Pop psychologists are forever advising "if you're in a job you don't like, get out of it." Easy for them to say. For many people, finding a fun job is simply not an option — there are simply not enough Ben and Jerry's taste tester jobs to go around.

However, for nearly everyone, there are parts of one's job that are enjoyable and parts that are wretched, parts that are stimulating and parts that are boring. In a perfect world, you would be able to delegate the drudge jobs and hold on to the exciting ones.

Unfortunately, this is not a perfect world. While there are many mundane tasks you, the center director, can delegate, there are certain ugly ones that you can't give away, ignore, or avoid. If you listen to the pop psychologists and only attend to the things you enjoy, you're setting your organization up for disaster.

If you don't fire a lousy teacher, her continuing presence will demotivate other teachers and deprive the children of the experiences they deserve. If you hate writing grant proposals, you may miss an opportunity to attract employer support for your center.

Your best bet is to get the ugly jobs out of the way right away. If you procrastinate on the uglies, even when you are working away at jobs you enjoy, this pleasure will be spoiled by the knowledge that the ugly work is still out there. So eat your cauliflower fast, then sit back and enjoy the Cherries Garcia.

Paradox #2
The more staff strive to protect you, the more they hurt you.

Many of us seem to have this need to take care of everyone. We want everyone to be happy, satisfied, productive, supported, connected. It takes a lot of time and energy to "Mother Hen" the world, but we do it because we need to.

So when the tables turn and staff want to take care of us, it can feel pretty good. It's certainly great to know that others are noticing when we are overburdened, that they see the magnitude of our responsibilities, that they are sensitive to the fact that a piece of information or news might *put us over the top.*

Though done with the best of intentions (of course this could also be done with less positive motivation), this protective behavior will ultimately prove harmful. There will be information missing, holes in the big picture — and this will hinder the effectiveness of your decision making. If you don't know that two staff members are not getting along, that a parent is upset about a staff comment, that the key to the storage unit is missing, that you are running out of peanut butter, things will fall apart when these specifics would inform your decision making.

Staff need to understand that you, as director, need to know everything. Their motivations for protection can be acknowledged and appreciated, while the act of protection can be firmly, continually rejected. Perhaps staff can learn to deliver the bad news with a gentle touch or a chocolate chip cookie (or would we come to fear cookies?).

Paradox #3
When you are most discouraged, you need to be most motivated.

Art Dronen, Roger's high school track coach, had only one piece of advice for all of us would-be heroes — "Ya gotta wanna." We, of course, treated this as trite nonsense. Decades later, Roger now sees that Art was a wise man.

His wisdom is best exemplified in the world of sports where typically athletes' success will in large part be determined by their determination to succeed. We all remember the Swiss female Olympic marathoner who stumbled into the Los Angles Coliseum totally exhausted. She staggered wildly and painfully about the oval, waving off the assistance of her coaches. Finally, she stumbled across the finish line and fell unconscious into the arms of a race official. She had been training for ten years to complete an Olympic marathon, and when her body gave out in total exhaustion 400 yards from the finish line, her sheer determination kept her going until her mission was accomplished.

While center directors are seldom cheered on by a spirited crowd of 100,000, they do frequently demonstrate amazing feats of perseverance. In fact, it is in the very nature of the director's job to be confronted, on an almost daily basis, with daunting challenges: replacing sick teachers at 6 am, dealing with an accusation of child abuse, juggling cash flow when reserves are depleted, finding a way to get children home from a field trip when the bus breaks down. Confronted with such frustrations, many directors throw in the towel; they either quit or quit caring.

The directors who succeed, and go on to manage the best programs, are those who don't cave in when the going gets tough, those who are determined, against all odds, to maintain a focus on delivering quality services. These directors have a "Ya gotta wanna" attitude that consistently carries them to the finish line.

Paradox #4
To accomplish the most serious results, you need to believe in the value of whimsy.

Never underestimate the value of humor. Why did laughter get the bad rap for indicating lack of seriousness, slacking off? Our staff meetings are great fun. When an outsider overhears the tone of our meetings, he or she will usually comment with something like: "There was so much laughing going on. How do you get anything done?"

It is the laughter that binds us together, that creates an environment and a sense of teamwork that enables people to share their joys and sorrows, as well as their frustrations and needs. People who can laugh at and with each other, trust each other.

Consider the staff meeting when we were in our usual stories with laughter mode and Roger arrived a bit late and announced: "We have a lot of work to get done today, so we'll just chit-chat for a few more minutes and then get down to it." Suddenly, no one had anything to say. We just sat around and ate our lunch and talked through the issues of the day. Laughter was minimized, as was the amount of work accomplished.

A playful approach to life issues, whether personal or professional, fosters creative potential, reduces stress, and just makes living a whole lot better.

Paradox #5
The longer you work, the less you are appreciated.

You were hired as director when the center was in the red and struggling to survive. You slashed expenditures to the bone, cracked down on late payments, built up enrollment, and got the center on the right track. Then you steadied the course when a disgruntled former teacher started spreading nasty false rumors; you kept the center going through a flu epidemic; and you even kept things afloat when a glitzy new center opened across the street.

Now you've been on the job 12 years and the center is running as smooth as can be. You naturally assume that, with all your heroic accomplishments in the past, you have a vast store of good will and credibility built up. Then you have to fire a popular teacher for valid reasons, but reasons you can't share with the staff. The teachers revolt and call for your resignation.

What happened to all that credibility? Since you single-handedly saved the center time and time again, why can't they give you the benefit of the doubt now?

The problem is that organizations have short memories. Given normal turnover, many of your teachers weren't even around when you were leaping tall buildings in a single bound. And those who were around, now that times are easier, tend to forget how stressful life was in the past. As a matter of fact, the longer your center sails along smoothly, the more staff may think your job has become a slam dunk, even though it is your brilliant management that is responsible for the good times.

Don't be too harsh on staff for their fickleness. Maybe you are contributing to the problem. Isn't it possible that after all those years of major stress, now you are content to settle into a mode of management that is steadying the course? Just maybe you've become a bit stodgy — reluctant to rock the boat, to try new ventures, to listen to new ideas, to tolerate parents or staff who don't fit a certain profile.

Longevity and credibility don't go hand in hand. Don't ever assume that you have so much good will built up that you can rest on your laurels. The relevant question is: "What have you done for the center and all its players lately that earns their appreciation?"

Paradox #6
Everyone's your friend when things are going well, but your true friends stand by you in the tough times.

When a crisis rears its ugly head, it is your support system that will save you. We have been rescued on many occasions by the concern and response of our friends — and that might very well include you.

Friends are not, in this case, the people who come up with all the platitudes: "This is really good for you." "Every cloud has a silver lining." "Everything works out in the end." People who say such things provide comfort and cry with you (or drive you crazy), but they don't pull you through.

Friends in crisis are the people who really put themselves into your problem, who put their minds and hearts into understanding where you are and what options you have. They are the people who say, "Have you tried… ?" "Why wouldn't this work… ?" "If other people can do this, why can't you… ?" "Here's an idea that might work…."

These are the people who will help you see your way out. They are the people who will expand the boundaries of your thinking, who will challenge you to use the skills you possess (which they might also remind you of). Be sure you have such friends around you. They are honest and blunt — essential and beyond value.

Bonnie Neugebauer

Bonnie Neugebauer is Editor of *Exchange Magazine* and a co-founder of the World Forum Foundation.

Roger Neugebauer

Roger Neugebauer is publisher of *Exchange Magazine* and a co-founder of the World Forum Foundation.

You Say Staff Deserve Respect?

Energize Your Words with Action!

by Karen Stephens

Whether they represent folks in rural areas or big cities, political leaders in the spotlight routinely pronounce children as our nation's greatest resource. And now with hard-core brain research echoing their claim, the "pols" pronounce even louder how vital quality early childhood programs are to our country's welfare. They couch their support in terms of investing in our future workforce, our future bevy of taxpayers. Rarely is it frankly said it's simply the right thing to do.

And so leaders continue to skirt comprehensive measures that would put money behind their rhetoric, behind our children and programs that serve them. You know the economic culture in the United States as well as I do. If one truly believes in something, they back it with greenbacks. So far, our nation has been mighty measly. We've yet to muster collective commitment to children.

And, by extension, our country has been measly with its child care providers. Oh sure, people of note now proclaim child care is a noble calling, not merely babysitting. (How long did it take us to get THAT idea across?!) And they publicly commend child care folks for the lasting contribution we make to society. Astute leaders even cite studies that reveal the best path to quality child care is to maintain a well-educated and trained staff.

But coming through with the resources to compensate quality caregivers — well that idea seems to cool as fast as news cameras' spotlights dim. Perhaps positive steps have been made in your program; but on a national scale, the necessity of taking a vow of poverty to work in child care still reigns.

So while you and I and our fellow child care directors wait for voters to hold leaders accountable for their rhetoric, we're left shouldering the task of maintaining a stable child care workforce for American families. You may say I'm being overly dramatic, even pessimistic. I say I'm being realistic.

So how do directors motivate professionals who are usually undercompensated (I'm talking minimum wage even with a four-year degree); their skills typically underestimated ("Oh, you're so lucky to sit around and play with kids all day"); and their commitment often discounted ("So when are you getting a real job?")?

I certainly don't have all the answers. In my 20+ years in child care, I've participated in innumerable salary surveys and equity wage initiatives. Some have even come through with meaningful results. But I still rarely see professionally trained child care providers paid as well as their public school counterparts.

I'm not naive. Even when better pay becomes a reality, it still takes more than money to motivate and retain well-qualified staff. In fact, all things being equal (if that ever happens), intrinsic motivation is far more influential on staff performance and longevity. And the proof is visible in child care programs everywhere. Considering the average child care provider makes less than $15,000 annually, I'm not amazed 40% of us leave the child care field annually; I'm amazed 60% of us stay in it! Intrinsic motivation is the key.

So, over the years, I've tried to come up with a plethora of tangible ways to help staff feel great about the job they're doing. To feel great in their hearts and minds. I've tried to show respect for their knowledge and to appreciate their talent. And I don't take for granted their dedication to children and families. Some strategies have been simple to carry out; others require more effort. And I must warn you, some may be hokey, but they've all been effective.

I'll share my ideas below. Hopefully, they'll trigger your own imagination. Despite the miles that distance us, together we can work to keep our nation's child care infrastructure — our staff — stable, experienced, motivated, and proud. Until child care professionals receive proper monetary compensation, the least we can do is feed their generous spirits with respect and appreciation.

Tangible Ways to Show Staff Respect and Appreciation

1. Post staff photos near entrance. Include position title, length of service, credentials, and brief biography.

2. Include staff profiles in program newsletters. Distribute newsletters not only to parents and your board, but also to program funders and supporters.

3. Include staff in community meetings whenever possible. Introduce them, with title, to *movers and shakers* in attendance. Recognize staff at appropriate events, such as program dedication ceremonies or other public functions.

4. Supply each staff member with a professional business card for networking purposes.

5. Post announcements for parents whenever staff acquire in-service training or renew certificates such as in first aid training.

6. Recommend qualified staff as workshop presenters and training consultants.

7. Send staff members' *parents* clippings of program news coverage. (Yes, I'm serious. No matter what your staff's age, she always like to make their parents proud.)

8. Send staff members' hometown newspapers press releases, such as announcements of your program's accreditation.

9. Publicly (as well as in evaluations) give staff credit for program improvements. If someone comes up with a creative idea or solution, they should bask in the glory!

10. Organize *regular* events for *team bonding*. Team spirit and camaraderie solidified when we instituted monthly staff dinners. It's a great tradition.

11. Recognize and utilize each staff member's unique talents. I have a teacher with a strong background in physical education. I turn to her for recommendations on new gross-motor equipment; she knows I count on her expertise. Another teacher is a wizard with children's computer

programs. She's our leader when purchasing decisions are made. AND she gets a subscription to a newsletter on children's software, so her input can be well informed. (Meaning, I try — even in small ways — to help her be successful in her job.)

12. Take time to regularly observe in classrooms. At least yearly, *write up* your observations for the room's staff to read within a few days. The speedy feedback is always appreciated. The process is time consuming, but it allows you to document for personnel files as well as to congratulate staff on skillful child guidance or inventive curriculum.

13. Provide one-on-one mentoring when possible. If not, try to find a mentor to fit a staff member's needs. Is a teacher having trouble arranging his environment? Help him with new arrangements or ask for another staff member's expertise.

14. Encourage staff members' hobbies and interests. Is a teacher into bunnies big time? Go ahead and buy a bunny windsock for her play yard. The kids will learn about wind and she'll appreciate the individualized attention.

15. Make copies of complimentary letters from parents for staff keepsakes.

16. Solicit staff input on decisions that affect them. For instance, they can identify best times to hold parent-teacher conferences.

17. Before preparing supplies and equipment budgets, ask staff to submit a list of recommended purchases.

18. Provide staff with articles, videos, or conference information that address topics of special interest. Are teachers interested in learning about the Project Approach? If so, secure funds to send them to a workshop. (My personal dream is to find travel funds so our teachers can visit the Reggio Emilia programs in Italy!)

19. Encourage staff to serve on professional boards and committees. Recognize their efforts when talking to staff, parents, and board members.

20. Compliment staff when they participate in wellness and stress management programs. Literally, they deserve a pat on the back for staying healthy!

21. Recognize staff talent in simple and spontaneous ways. When I go to a conference, I bring something back from the exhibitor's venue. One year, my treasures included a white rabbit puppet that popped out of a magician's black hat. I left the puppet as a surprise on the teachers' desks. An attached note said I marveled at the magic they do with kids. Yes, it's sappy and sentimental, but the teachers appreciated the thought all the same — and who doesn't need another puppet for the classroom?

22. Provide staff with as much personal space for organization and planning as possible. In days of old, our teachers had lockers, not an office. We've made a bit of progress since then, but not lots. Now four head teachers share a cramped office with one desk, a file cabinet, and a computer. Their office has a loveseat for comfort, but also stores our children's library, two refrigerators, and its walls are stacked — literally to the ceiling — with *junk* supplies creative teachers love to squirrel away. They don't have the separate workstations, staff lounge, or make-it/take-it resource room of their dreams, but they know I'd jump for space that would give it to them.

23. Provide staff time to observe other programs. Mutually decide with staff where they'll observe, why, and when. Arrange for substitutes, so staff can leave without burdening those left with the kids.

24. Once a year, take a *fun and interesting* retreat or staff trip together. Visit an outstanding children's museum or go hear a famous children's author speak. Staff will appreciate the time you take to facilitate and organize their enjoyment.

25. Committed caregivers get a lot of enjoyment out of being partners with parents as they nurture children's development. To provide time for the communication the partner requires, bring in extra staff or volunteers at the beginning and

ending of the day (that's when parents are most likely to be in the classroom).

26. Bring in a bouquet of wildflowers or a new compact disc to classrooms *just because.* Employees and children respond to aesthetics.

27. Involve staff in any changes in their work environment. We recently renovated one of our site's play yard. I can't tell you how many times I volleyed construction ideas between architects and teaching staff. I continually asked if a purposed design would help or hinder our teachers' job performance. And boy did it pay off! Our program ended up with a much better play yard because the people who used it day in and day out provided guidance. And the staff were pleased to be included in making decisions with other professionals. (In truth, they prevented the committee from making numerous design mistakes!)

28. Serve on committees that organize a community-wide child care provider recognition day. If there isn't one already, start one yourself. Staff will note your efforts to celebrate the important work they do.

29. Teachers love books. Make it a program practice to treat them with birthday or holiday gift certificates for a bookstore. Whether they purchase a book for relaxation or for reading to the children, your program will win either way.

30. Occasionally surprise teachers with helpful supplies that are tools of the trade. This could be a big-ticket item, like a laminating machine. But most likely your budget will better afford something simple, like notepads with motivational sayings. "To teach is to touch the future" is a perennial favorite.

31. Encourage and facilitate your program staff and parents' involvement with Worthy Wage Day!

32. Buy each program site a subscription to the newsletter *Rights, Raises and Respect* — the biannual publication of the National Center for Early Childhood Workforce, $30/year. Send fee to: NCECW, 733 15th Street NW, Suite 1037, Washington, DC 20005-2112.

33. Nominate deserving staff for awards bestowed by the community or profession.

34. Ask staff for recommendations of curriculum books to add to their resource library. (And if they don't have an on-site resource library, create one. Our staff's resource library is located in my office.)

35. Reimburse staff for part or all of their professional dues to organizations, such as local affiliates of the National Association for the Education of Young Children (to identify your local, call 800-424-2460).

36. Reimburse staff for part or all of continuing education costs, whether they be through conferences or college classes. Be sure to recognize staff each time they complete a course that improves their job skills.

So there you are, 36 tangible and specific ways to value your staff and the life-affirming work they perform. As you put these ideas into practice, you'll put action behind your hopes and dreams for children. It's the ethical thing to do — the right thing to do. And may the rest of the world follow your lead.

Karen Stephens

Karen Stephens, M.S. in education specializing in early childhood, began her career as a teacher in a preschool classroom in 1975. From 1980 to May 2013 she served as campus child care director and taught child development and early childhood program administration courses for the Illinois State University's Department of Family and Consumer Sciences. Today she writes from her home and enjoys occasional travel to deliver staff development training and conference presentations.

Becoming an Authentic Communicator

by Johnna Darragh Ernst

We are constantly communicating. From the moment we wake 'til our day comes to a close, we send and receive messages. These messages impact our ability to form meaningful connections with others. Early childhood professionals use communication to form meaningful relationships with children, with their families, and with colleagues. Communication is such an incredibly important skill, yet one that's often taken for granted.

Stopping to meaningfully reflect on and develop communication skills might be something that's done when communication goes awry — perhaps you are struggling in a relationship with a coworker, or maybe you just don't feel that you are connecting with the parent of a child in your class. Pausing and thinking about communication at these times can assist with problem solving and potential conflict resolution. However, mindfully reflecting on your contributions to communication exchanges and brushing up on foundational skills before challenges arise can sharpen your capacity to serve as a communication partner and enhance the connections you make with others.

What does it mean to truly connect with someone else? Is connection merely having your messages understood and understanding the messages of another? Or is the goal of connection deeper than

that? One possible goal is that of authenticity — where communication is infused with integrity and empathy and your interactions represent your truest, most powerful self. According to Brown (2010), authenticity emerges from a sense of personal worthiness and courage. Authenticity creates a climate of respect. When you communicate authentically, others can communicate from a space that represents their truest, most powerful selves.

Unfortunately, there are many daily roadblocks to authentic communication. Distraction is a big culprit: you might have a long list of things to do on your mind, and on your desk a cell phone constantly dinging with the pressing concerns of others, and an ever-busy and bustling classroom. Multiple things require your attention at the same time. Learning to practice *mindfulness* in communication is an important first step toward authenticity.

Mindfulness

Naomi is talking with the parent of a three year old in her class. The parent is concerned that her child is not engaging with her peers. The conversation is taking place during morning drop-off, and Naomi is having a hard time focusing. Naomi is aware of several other parents who are waiting to talk with her. Although her co-teacher is creating an engaging environment for the children in the classroom, Naomi is struggling with the desire to quickly end the conversation.

Situations like Naomi's are common — one individual within a communication exchange might have a very important message to convey, but time and place for the communication partner is problematic. Finding time for a more in-depth discussion is necessary. Prior to deciding if additional time and another place for conversation is needed, it is important to mindfully participate in the communication exchange. Mindful communication requires being *fully present* and *attending*. When you are *fully present*:

■ you are in the moment, blocking out distractors. Your mind is alert and in tune to your communication partner.

■ your body communicates your interest — you lean in slightly with open arms, nodding your head at appropriate intervals.

■ you work to clear your mind of all but the message being conveyed.

■ you are open to the possibilities that the communication exchange brings.

When you are *attending*:

■ you focus on the message that your communication partner is conveying.

■ you listen with your ears and eyes, taking in words as well as non-verbal messages.

■ you actively work to suspend judgment about the messages you are receiving.

Being fully present and attending requires accepting responsibility for your contributions to the exchange and recognizing that outcomes are based on your understanding the messages conveyed.

For Naomi, being mindful will enable her to understand the parent's viewpoint. Naomi can then respond to the parent from a space that reflects that understanding, communicating respect. Should further exploration and an in-depth discussion be needed, she can suggest an alternative time to meet.

A lack of mindfulness risks mindlessness. According to Dan Huston, author of *Communicating Mindfully* (2010), mindlessness contributes to missed opportunities: opportunities to make connections and learn what others are thinking; opportunities to explore new solutions to problems; opportunities to represent your best self; and opportunities to convey respect for your communication partner.

Authentic communication requires much more than understanding the messages of others. Communication is a complex, bi-directional, and emotional process. During communication, we work to understand the messages of others, and often have emotional reactions to these messages. Your reactions to these messages might be positive, negative, or neutral.

Naomi, for example, will have her own perceptions about what the parent is communicating; perhaps she has similar concerns about the child. Or maybe she has not noticed the child's challenges in the classroom. She might interpret the parent's concern as anxiety or even question why the parent is so concerned. For Naomi to engage in authentic communication, it's important that she recognize her perceptions and their impact on her reactions.

Another important skill in authentic communication, therefore, is learning to *explore existing perceptions*.

Exploring Existing Perceptions

Perceptions are our reactions to the messages we receive, and can provide explanations for events or the actions of others. One of the challenges that exists with communication is that our perceptions are not always accurate: they are strongly shaped by unique schemas that are developed based on past experiences. Schemas represent mental structures that consist of related bits of information; we put these bits of information together, and develop larger and more complex patterns of meaning (O'Hair & Weineman, 2009). Schemas, as accepted storylines, can be very beneficial as they tell us what to generally expect in interactions. For example, when I pick up the phone and say, "Hello," I expect that someone will respond. As schemas represent general expectations, we don't necessarily think of them or recognize that we have them. It's not until these unwritten codes or expectations are violated that we even realize we had expectations for how things would proceed.

Just as they can be beneficial, schemas can also be limiting. Schemas can create *selective perception*, where an automatic interpretation of the situation replaces an authentic evaluation (O'Hair & Weineman, 2009). For example, imagine that Naomi has a schema, or storyline, that the parent she is interacting with is always expressing a concern regarding her child's development. Naomi feels that these concerns are not warranted. Naomi, because of this schema, may be less likely to truly focus on what the parent is saying.

As schemas are often automatic, we may not even recognize we are applying them. When confronted with data that contradicts our existing schemas, we often do one of two things: disregard the contradicting information or change our schema. If we continuously disregard contradictory information, our schemas can be inaccurate. The storylines we create become out of sync with emerging information and the realities of others (Huston, 2010).

If Naomi typically disregards the parent's concerns, but can acknowledge now that she has an existing schema, her careful attention to the mother's concerns could guide her to a new understanding. If she were to examine her perceptions, Naomi would investigate the issue more closely and observe the child in the classroom. Perhaps Naomi will learn from the mother that her daughter is not connecting with other children outside of class. Are there possible connections with other children and families that Naomi can help this child and family make? If Naomi does not move beyond her initial schema, she will never know if her initial reaction is accurate or

inaccurate, and could miss additional information and opportunities to connect with and support this family.

Learning about your existing schemas involves carefully listening to your reactions. During a communication exchange, stop and focus inward: What is your internal voice saying? You may catch yourself thinking, "Well, he always..." or "That is just how she reacts..." or "Isn't that just typical?" These thoughts reflect assumptions. Assumptions are often based on faulty schemas and can contribute to selective perception: we see behaviors that fit our expectations. For example, if you always expect a parent to express disapproval during your interactions, you are likely to look for that behavior and disregard interactions where that behavior doesn't occur. When we make assumptions, we stop looking for why certain behaviors might be happening and operate based on storylines that we have in our heads. Learning to look beyond this automatic response creates an opportunity to search for accurate explanations free of existing perceptions and schemas. This is referred to as *adopting a clean-slate perspective*.

Adopting a Clean-slate Perspective

Clean-slate perspectives free us from existing schemas (Brown & Richard, 2003). Each interaction becomes a new opportunity to connect without existing bias. In each communication exchange:

- you carefully tune in to your communication partner.

- you are fully aware of your own perceptions and schemas.

- you have the ability to make choices mindfully about your reactions based on the information presented.

- you are truly open to communication as you are invested in the exchange.

To adopt a clean-slate perspective, it's important to:

■ practice mindfulness, and actively tune in to what the other individual is saying.

■ learn to listen to your own perceptions:

- What information do they give you about your own schemas and potential biases?

- How might these perceptions influence your interactions?

■ choose to respond based on a clean slate, where you consider the information in front of you as opposed to previously acquired assumptions that may or may not be accurate.

It's important to note that some schemas can be very beneficial in the context of communication. For example, we have schemas that inform us about preferred modes of communication, and schemas that provide us with information that we use in the context of relationships. There are, however, schemas that can detract from meaningful connection. These can often emerge from previous interactions that we have perceived as challenging. It is these schemas that benefit most from reexamination. Let's check in with Naomi one last time.

Naomi adopts a clean-slate perspective when she frees her mind from thinking that the mother is acting in a way that reflects her ungrounded concerns about her daughter. Instead, she truly listens to what the mother has to say. Naomi is now approaching the interaction without her previous biases. She gathers information that she can then respond to; this information is not clouded by a lens that has pre-disposed her to disregard what the mother has to say.

Take a moment to consider your own goals for connection. How do your daily communication skills and strategies support your overall goals? Reflect on how being mindful, exploring existing perceptions, and adopting a clean-slate perspective might deepen your ability to authentically communicate and connect with others, thereby deepening the relationships of those you interact with on a daily basis.

References

Brown, B. (2010). The power of vulnerability. Ted Talk. Available at: www.ted.com/talks/brene_brown_on_vulnerability/transcript?language=en#t-467000

Brown, K., & Richard R. (2003). The benefits of being present: Mindfulness and its role in psychological well-being. *Journal of Personality and Social Psychology, 84*(4), 822-848.

Huston, D. (2010). *Communicating mindfully: Mindfulness-based communication and emotional intelligence.* Independence, KY: Cengage Learning.

O'Hair, D. & Wiemann, M. (2009). *Real communication: An introduction.* New York: Bedford/St. Martin's.

Johnna Darragh Ernst

Dr. Johnna Darragh Ernst is a Professor of Early Childhood Education at Heartland Community College in Normal, Illinois, and serves as a faculty liaison to their Heartland's inclusive Child Development Lab. She is the author of several articles and two books, most recently, *The Welcoming Classroom: Building Strong Home-to-School Connections for Early Learning*, which focuses on communication and collaboration skills supporting family engagement. Johnna is also extensively involved in workforce development public policy work in Illinois.

Building and Rebuilding Your Credibility

by Roger Neugebauer

"What happened to my credibility?" pondered Kathryn. Kathryn had been hired as director of the Hill Street Child Care Center when it was in crisis. The center was broke, its license had just been revoked, and two long-time teachers had just left to start their own center — taking many parents with them. Tempted to quit when she found out how bad the crisis was, Kathryn decided to give it a shot. She worked 60-hour weeks, doing everything from tearing down the old porch (that had cost the center its license) to teaching the three-year-old class, cooking meals, and driving all over town posting ads for teachers and parents.

After two years, the center was back on its feet; three years later, Kathryn had the center accredited with a long waiting list.

Then one day she observed a teacher hitting a child. In accordance with center policies, she dismissed the teacher immediately. Also in accord with center policies, Kathryn could not disclose to parents or teachers the reason for the termination.

Unfortunately, the dismissed teacher was very popular, and she felt no compunction about spreading the story that she was terminated because the director was jealous of her popularity. Pandemonium ensued; teachers were in revolt, and parents threatened to withdraw.

Over the weeks that it took to put out this fire, Kathryn couldn't help but wonder why, after sacrificing everything to save the center, she seemed to lose all her credibility in one afternoon.

Was her predicament fair? Of course not. Was her predicament unusual? Unfortunately not.

For center directors, establishing credibility with teachers and parents is not a one-time event. Credibility must be continuously built and rebuilt. To understand why this is so, it is necessary to understand that establishing credibility is based upon meeting mutual expectations.

What Teachers Expect of a Center Director

■ **Staff expect you to be an expert.** Staff respect a director who knows her stuff, who really understands how to deliver quality child care. They need to know that if they have a problem they can turn to the director and know they will get the support and guidance they need.

■ **Staff expect you to know what's going on.** The most frequently voiced complaint about bosses is that they are out of touch with what is happening on the floor. A director loses credibility when teachers perceive (whether correctly or not) that he doesn't understand (or care about) the day-to-day issues they face.

■ **Staff expect you to make good decisions.** Most decisions a director makes involve a mix of financial, organizational, and tactical factors, factors that few staff are aware of. For staff to have confidence in their director, they must trust that she is balancing all these factors wisely and making decisions that are in the best interests of the organization.

■ **Staff expect you to listen.** Nothing is more demotivating than to believe that others do not respect your judgment. Teachers need to believe that the director values their opinions and takes their input (whether requested or volunteered) seriously.

■ **Staff expect you to be fair.** In order for staff to respect you, they need to be convinced that you

will treat them fairly when it comes to scheduling, raises, discipline, and attention.

So you can see that there are many areas where a director can slip up and not meet staff expectations, causing a lapse in credibility. But if a director is working hard to meet staff expectations, she can legitimately have certain expectations of her teachers.

What Center Directors Expect of Teachers

■ **Directors expect teachers to be committed to the organization.** You have the right to expect teachers to be loyal to your organization, to behave professionally at work during good times and bad, and to represent the organization well in the community.

■ **Directors expect teachers to communicate concerns.** The hardest problems to solve are those you don't know about. Teachers may think they are doing you a favor by withholding bad news (about an upset parent, a child having trouble, or equipment not working); but by depriving you of the opportunity to fix a problem early, they run the risk of it turning into a crisis. For you to succeed, you depend upon staff to share concerns and problems before they are out of control.

■ **Directors expect teachers to trust them.** Since you cannot consult every teacher about every decision you make, you need for them to trust your judgment, to give you the benefit of the doubt. If you are looking over your shoulder worrying about how staff will perceive every decision, your effectiveness will be undermined.

What You Can Do to Maintain Credibility

You are not at the mercy of fate when it comes to maintaining your credibility. You can take an active hand in improving your credibility with some basic common sense actions:

■ **Don't fool yourself.** Don't expect that the credibility you have earned from your heroic efforts in the past will last forever. If you take your credibility for granted, you may be in for a big surprise, much as the one that Kathryn experienced. Staff and parents have short memories when it comes to director accomplishments.

■ **Keep current.** Your bachelor's degree in child development may have been state-of-the-art in 1975, but in case you haven't noticed, the field has moved on a bit since then. I still remember my third grade teacher, Mrs. Boetchen, who taught the same lesson plan on the same day year after year for her entire career. Those first few years it was probably an exciting class, but by the time I came on the scene, it was a bit tedious.

Directors can fall into the same rut, assuming their understanding of child development will hold for decades and as a result allowing their center to fall behind the times. You need to keep on top of new ideas in child and family development or you will not remain on top.

■ **Keep visible.** If staff never see you in the classrooms, they will naturally assume you are out of touch. Setting aside specific times every week where you visit classrooms may or may not get you up to speed on the day-to-day issues facing teachers, but it will go a long way toward keeping staff assured that you have your finger on the pulse of the center.

■ **Be fair.** Leadership textbooks instruct leaders in training to be scrupulously evenhanded in dealing with staff. "Don't play favorites" are the standard words to the wise. What the textbooks fail to tell you is that in real life you will have favorites. There will be some staff you absolutely worship and others you tolerate only because they seem to hit it off with the children and parents.

If you have such feelings, don't feel guilty — this is normal. What is abnormal, and destructive, is if you let your emotions dictate your treatment of

staff — if you are always bending the rules to help the teachers you like and enforcing the letter of the law for those you don't. Once staff members perceive that you grant 'most favored teacher' status to an in-crowd, your credibility is on the skids.

■ **Keep staff in the loop.** Fear of the unknown erodes confidence. Staff become insecure when they feel they don't know where their center is headed and what that means for them. Timely information can reduce most of this anxiety.

Many center directors are martyrs who like to carry all the burdens on their shoulders. If the center is losing enrollment and cash flow projections are troubling, such a director shields her staff from this scary news, hoping to resolve the situation before staff even learn about it. The problem with this line of thinking is that staff usually sense something is wrong and without firm information start worrying about worst-case scenarios.

Just as you do not want staff to protect you by withholding bad news, you should not be overly protective of your staff. Keep them in the loop about where the center is headed, about developments — good and bad. Particularly when change is on the way — when funding is about to be cut, when you are contemplating adding a new classroom, when you are thinking about redoing the schedule — prepare staff early for the change ahead.

■ **Don't overstay your welcome.** Not all loss of credibility is subject to repair. At some point in your career, it is possible that staff may start losing confidence in you because you in fact are starting to lose your enthusiasm, or because you are starting to lose your ability to keep up with changes.

The problem is, if you are starting to lose your edge on the job, you are likely to be the last person to know this. While staff will complain freely to each other that you have lost some of your fire and savvy, they may be reluctant to share this feedback with you.

If you have been the director in one place for a long time, you need to find a confidant (someone on your board or maybe an outside consultant) who can evaluate your performance and give you honest feedback. If your confidant reports that your performance is starting to tail off, this indeed may be a sign that it is time to give serious consideration to moving on.

More likely, it may simply be a warning that you need to revitalize your commitment. There may be steps you can take to regain your edge. You can:

- change your focus from the day-to-day to the long range — pouring energy into developing a long-range plan for the organization.

- spend some time visiting other centers, both near and far, to get new ideas and to re-stimulate your creativity.

- change your role, turning over administrivia to a trusted assistant, and working less hours as the educational leader.

- recruit a sister center in another nation so that you, the teachers, and the children can enjoy the insights of communicating with peers in a different setting.

- start writing articles for Exchange.

Whatever you do, don't take your credibility for granted. Take the initiative — it will not only strengthen your rapport with staff, but it may renew you enthusiasm.

Roger Neugebauer

Roger Neugebauer is publisher of *Exchange Magazine* and a co-founder of the World Forum Foundation.

If Your Boss Is the Problem, What Choices Do You Have?

by Holly Elissa Bruno

"I have learned that courage was not the absence of fear, but the triumph over it. The brave person is not s/he who does not feel afraid, but s/he who conquers that fear."

Nelson Mandela

A Scary Question to Ask

Saying out loud, "What do I do if my boss is the problem?" can be risky. To lessen the danger in asking this question, most people survey the environment first to make certain no one else is listening. Foreboding in the form of shortness of breath, pounding heart, and terror of repercussions crowds in on the person who needs an answer.

I don't have enough fingers and toes to count the times I have been asked by teachers and administrators: "What do I do if my boss is the problem?"

Thankfully, saying this question out loud to someone you trust is also alleviating. The next question is: "What, if anything, can I do to make things better?" Asking these scary questions is the first step to finding help.

Scary Behavior by the Boss

As I listen to each person's concern about her boss, I hear that the boss is:

- encouraging others to complain to the boss rather than working things through with the employee who's asking the question.

- fostering a culture of gossip and negativity so no one knows whom to trust.

- reversing decisions made by the employee and thereby harming that employee's credibility and authority.

- micromanaging every decision, causing others to be fearful of taking action.

- unpredictable, temperamental.

- manipulative.

- unresponsive and unavailable (emotionally, physically, spiritually, or all of these).

- verbally abusive.

- prone to yelling; threatening.

- shaming, blaming, or both.

- telling people whatever they want to hear and anything but the truth.

- totally 'political,' doing whatever is needed to hold on to power.

- throwing employees 'under the nearest bus' to take the fall for the boss.

- unwilling or unable to make tough decisions.

- just plain 'off the wall.'

- other_____ .

Sound familiar to you? If you need to add more 'scary boss' traits to the list, I've left you space!

Many of us have worked for a bad boss or may well deal with one in the future. As educators responsible for offering children, families, and our programs our heartfelt and mindful best, we need a boss who 'gets' us, helps us grow professionally, treats us with respect and fairness, and has our backs. We do not need a saboteur. Nor do we do need a power struggle. Power struggles are far from the most mature way to handle workplace conflict. No one wins a power struggle. Even the 'winner' has a new enemy.

Take a look at the dilemma director LaDonna faces. How would you advise her to address the issues with her boss, Marietta?

LaDonna's Challenge: Who's the Boss at Children's Safe Harbor?

Children's Safe Harbor Child Development Center was founded by Marietta 35 years ago. Safe Harbor's enrollment has steadily grown, the number of staff has quadrupled, and six years ago, a sparkling new facility opened its doors.

Two months ago Marietta finally hired a director, an action her board had urged for at least a decade. Marietta's new title of Executive Director came with a large bright office and a vague job description of 'overseeing program operations' while 'supervising

the Director.' Board Chair, James, would have preferred that Marietta retire.

Troubles began before LaDonna walked through the door. Marietta, life-long personal friends with many staff members, assured staff she wasn't really leaving; they could always come to her. She'd see them on the weekends, at church on Sunday, and at the beauty parlor. Marietta said, "Call me anytime — night or day."

LaDonna, upbeat and enthusiastic, had been successful as an Assistant Director of a center across town; so, she was confident Safe Harbor was a good fit. James advised LaDonna that Safe Harbor needed new blood and fresh ideas; both the curriculum and staff policies were out-of-date and the staff lacked proper supervision. Parents were complaining that their children were bored.

LaDonna began by meeting with each team member individually, listening to her hopes and needs for the future, as well as to any concerns. She came away from these sessions feeling that more recently hired teachers would welcome change; but, many of the 'old guard' would need time to adjust.

At her first staff meeting, LaDonna shared the overall results of these interviews and noted that the majority of teachers wanted to try new approaches in their classrooms. She offered alternative curricula and invited teachers to share their ideas in small groups. Everyone appeared to be on board.

Little did she know that Marietta's closest friends on staff complained to Marietta immediately: "I'm not changing the way I teach; I've taught this way for 20 years! The children love me." Other long-time members of the staff agreed, upon Marietta's prompting, that LaDonna was pushy. Marietta told them not to worry; she would straighten LaDonna out. Of course, everyone knew that Marietta handles conflict indirectly.

By the end of LaDonna's first month, Safe Harbor is anything but safe. Teachers have formed exclusive cliques loyal to either LaDonna or Marietta. Some teachers outright tell LaDonna: "Marietta told me I didn't have to make any changes." Others smirk when LaDonna visits their classrooms and makes recommendations. LaDonna asked to meet with Marietta to get everything out on the table. When they met, Marietta suggested, with a smile, that LaDonna must be imagining things. Marietta felt confident the Board will come crawling to have her return as Director.

And there you have it: a power struggle rages beneath the surface. Can the children feel it? You bet they can. Will anything help when the boss, like Marietta, is the problem? Or, are we stuck like flies on sticky paper?

For help with this dilemma, I interviewed three groups of experts and expert practitioners on the topic:

■ Jack Gabarro, Harvard Business School professor and author of *Managing Your Boss* (2005) and *Hechinger Report* author Justin Snider;

■ Robert Sutton, Stanford professor and author of *Good Boss: Bad Boss* (2006);

■ Brandi Pritchett-Johnson, University of Florida counseling and ethnicity expert;

■ Dwight Johnson, elementary school principal; Marquita Davis, executive director of a large community agency in Alabama; and,

■ Cori Berg, an early childhood director in Texas.

You can listen to each of these interviews, now podcasts, at www.hollyelissabruno.com or BAMradionetwork.com, "Leadership Strategies" by entering the name of any one of these guests.

Good Boss, Bad Boss: What Makes the Difference?

Let's get clear on what distinguishes a good boss from a bad one. You know what makes a boss good or bad for you. LaDonna is finding out.

To put your experience in context, consider emotional intelligence expert, Daniel Goleman's (2006) comparison of the traits and behaviors of both types of bosses (p. 277).

GOOD BOSS	BAD BOSS
■ Shows empathy	■ Self-centered
■ Decisive	■ Indecisive
■ Takes responsibility	■ Blames
■ Humble	■ Arrogant
■ Shares authority	■ Mistrusts
■ Great listener	■ Blank wall
■ Encourager	■ Doubter
■ Communicator	■ Secretive
■ Courageous	■ Intimidating
■ Sense of humor	■ Can't lighten up

Bob Sutton cautions that even the best bosses have an 'inner jerk' — that part of themselves that loses touch due to 'power poisoning.' To reverse this dynamic, Sutton suggests that leaders pay a bounty of $20 to any staff member who has the courage to tell the boss when the boss is misbehaving.

Let's compare the characteristics of good and bad bosses with research findings on characteristics of the leader as mentor (DeLong, Gabarro & Lees, 2008, p. 4). A good mentor:

- is someone absolutely credible whose integrity transcends the message, be it positive or negative. tells you things you may not want to hear, but leaves you feeling you have been heard.

- interacts with you in a way that makes you want to become better.

- makes you feel secure enough to take risks.

- gives you the confidence to rise above your inner doubts and fears.

- supports your attempts to set stretch goals for yourself.

- presents opportunities and highlights challenges you might not have seen on your own.

When Your Boss is Bad, What Can You Do?

Jack Gabarro, Harvard Business School professor's take on "What do you do if your boss is the problem" is twofold:

- Step back to evaluate and address what you bring to the conflict.

- Don't go over your boss's head unless you have a virtually 100% chance of success.

Gabarro encourages us to assess ourselves, the employee, first by asking:

- What behaviors of mine might tick off my boss?

- Am I focusing on what the boss (and our organization) needs as much as I am on my own needs?

- Am I expecting the impossible from any human being?

Gabarro advises us, "If you're having a problem with your boss, it is seldom all one-sided.... Start off with the premise that you are contributing some percentage of the problem, if for no other reason [than] because you don't understand who your boss is, what her strengths and weaknesses are, what his style or preferences [are] for receiving information or discussing either problematic or sensitive issues..." (Justin Snider's blog).

Gabarro reminds us that bosses have unique needs. Specifically, bosses have preferred ways of getting information. Some bosses need to hear the facts; other bosses need a big picture perspective. Some bosses want you to offer solutions. Other bosses want you to solve problems yourself and leave the boss alone. To determine your boss's needs, ask her direct questions like: "How do you need me to work with you?" and "What do you expect of me?" Gabarro encourages us: Put yourself in your boss's shoes: What does she or he need from you to be able to steer the organization?

Cleaning Up Your Part of the Problem

This empathetic approach to your boss helps you:

- find ways to speak your boss's language.

- place your needs in a larger perspective.

- 'get over yourself' if you are expecting your boss to be perfect.

Everyone needs something from the boss. How can you distinguish yourself by placing the organization's needs first, rather than focusing only on your situation? Gabarro's point makes sense if the employee is able to honestly assess herself and accept that her response to the boss may contribute to the problem. Gabarro's approach falters if the boss is a tyrant. A tyrant is a tyrant.

Make Sure the Stars are in Alignment if You Go Over Your Boss's Head

I asked Jack Gabarro: "Is going over your boss's head ever appropriate?" What if your boss really is the problem, and no amount of your hard work and/or changed behavior or attitude can make that right? My question stopped the conversation. Gabarro's response was the equivalent of a police siren: Don't go over your boss's head unless you have "all your stars in alignment. You'll pay for it one way or another."

Commentator Justin Snider, also a guest on my radio program, summarized this end-run tactic in his blog: "Gabarro and I agreed that going over your boss's head to complain about him or her doesn't often end well, though it may sometimes seem like the only option." The message: When your boss is the problem, put up, shut up (or get out). This is not what most employees want to hear. The advice sounds like a prescription for workplace servitude. By choosing to 'go along to get along' with a problematic boss, you have to accept or at least put up with offensive behavior. When an employee's dignity or integrity is under attack, this stick-it-out approach comes with too heavy a cost. At the least, the employee will feel resentful and demoralized. The worst case is burnout, illness and/or depression. The conflict, if left unresolved, will likely result in the employee's getting fired. Bosses don't like putting up with difficult employees, either.

Confronting the Boss: Being Honest About the Problem

Wouldn't it be wondrous if every boss could listen to her employees' feedback with an open mind and without taking negative feedback personally? Do you know bosses like that? If you do, you can take the direct approach: tell your boss what the problem is and offer (and request) alternative solutions that would work for you, the boss, and the organization. Be open to the boss's point of view and her solutions.

Even if your boss has difficulty dealing with conflict or negative feedback, you can still attempt to rework your relationship with her. Consider the step-by-step process below.

Steps to Taking the Direct Approach with Your Boss When Your Boss is the Problem

Prepare yourself:

- **Examine and clarify your intention:** What do you need most out of the meeting? What are you willing to accept? What are the deal-breakers?

- **Drop the attitude:** Leave at the door (even legitimate) feelings of resentment, hurt, martyrdom, blame, or shame.

- **Do damage control:** Prepare for the worst case scenario. What would you do if you lose your job? Can you at least make sure you get a severance package and/or a good reference?

Set up the meeting and environment for success:

- When you request a meeting with your boss, be direct and respectful about the purpose of the meeting.

- Agree on a time when you can talk without interruption.

- Set an agenda with time limitations.

- If possible, arrange to meet in a neutral off-site location like a quiet and private booth or table at a restaurant.

- Agree on the process you will use to resolve differences including the 'we agree to disagree' option.

Hold the meeting:

■ As objectively as you can, tell your boss what you need in order to perform your job to the best of your ability. Be clear about the barriers that detract from your performance.

■ Give concrete examples.

■ Ask your boss what she or he needs from you in order to work effectively together.

■ Discuss what changes each one of you can and is willing to make.

■ Agree on next steps.

■ If appropriate, end the meeting by stating one thing you honestly appreciate/value about the other person: something you would miss if you no longer worked together.

■ Alternatively, if the meeting proves useless, decide how you can gracefully bring it to an end. Manage your frustration level to avoid getting into a screaming match.

Debrief the meeting:

■ What went well?

■ What didn't feel right?

■ What did you both learn about one another that will help in future interactions?

■ If the meeting was a failure, what are your choices now?

■ Document the important decisions made at the meeting as soon as possible.

Worst Case Scenario:

A Mutually Respectful Conversation isn't Going to Happen Because the Boss Really is the Problem

This is the situation most employees find themselves in: for whatever reason, a heart-to-heart and/or meeting of the minds is not going to happen. This is painful for anyone. Who wants to deal with the potential disruption to your personal and professional life, not getting the recommendation you need, wondering if anyone will hire you if you can't get along with your boss, concern about paying your bills or uprooting your family? For many employees, these disruptions are overwhelming.

Even in this worst case scenario, you have choices.

Stay at the job, doing what you can in your own domain. Change your expectations. Limit (but don't avoid) interactions with your boss. Get realistic. Set aside the expectation that you will come to a meeting of the minds. Instead, manage your boundaries as well as you can. Be sure to accomplish everything in your job description, and document your actions.

Keep your boss informed. Document conversations with your boss. Much as you might need to, do not bad-mouth the boss to others. That insubordination qualifies you for termination and demoralizes other staff.

Share only with a trusted confidant who will help you find ways to deal with a less-than-ideal workplace relationship. Beware of characterizing your boss as a red-eyed, fire-breathing, employee-devouring cartoon character devil. Even the worst boss is human with some redeeming qualities. Keeping a balanced perspective in the most painful situations will prevent you from casting yourself in a holier-than-thou victim position. Victims have no power to make things better.

Staying on the job works if your job is meaningful enough for you to make the sacrifice of working without a boss's support and encouragement. In early childhood, most teachers or administrators who decide to stay at the organization do so because they love the children and their coworkers. Or, we stay on for personal reasons: our children are enrolled at the center; we need the income; no other jobs are available; we can't relocate.

You also need ways to release anxiety. Get stress out of your body before stress becomes toxic. Go outside. Walk it off. Surround yourself with beauty. Do things you love. Do acts of kindness, not just for others, but for yourself. You'll need to continuously restore yourself if your boss is the problem.

Find Yourself a Better Job and Resign

Your alternative to sticking out a bad situation is to vamoose. When you have done what is within your power to work things out and the situation remains unhealthy for you, move on. Scary as this is, getting sick, getting fired, and/or burning out are scarier possibilities.

Cut your losses. Build a larger network. Do the legwork of finding other happier positions. Move on as soon as you can. In time, you will find peace.

"We often look so long and so regretfully at the door that closes, we don't see the door that is opening for us."

Thomas Edison

Stepping out of a toxic relationship will be your first reward. If you make this choice, may the spiritual principle work for you: Close one door so that another can open.

"Have enough courage to trust love one more time and always one more time."

Maya Angelou

The Cross-cultural Challenge: Complication or Growth Opportunity?

Employee-boss ruptures are even more complex when cultural differences are part of the challenge. In early childhood, in particular, when white women manage black women, painful cultural histories can literally color the relationship. Dr. Brandi Pritchett-Johnson encourages us to examine our cultural history for baggage that jams up current workplace dynamics. She suggests that both employee and boss ask themselves together: "What (part of the problem) is 'my stuff'? Is this 'our stuff'? How are we going to get through this together?" Workplace rules of conduct can be very different for women of each culture.

Pritchett-Johnson cautions that black women, especially as leaders, often face unspoken negative expectations about their competency. A black leader will be challenged in her authority and feel she has to prove herself. Dr. Marquita Davis advises us all to discern who we are, share personal stories, become real so that "we laugh, we talk, we cry." When we become individuals and not a stereotype, we stand a far better chance of resolving differences. "Let them see who you are," urges Marquita. Once you have done that, you can make "deliberate opportunities to create relationships" that function well.

This does not mean that we deny our differences. Studies continuously show that when we delude ourselves into thinking, "We're all the same," we are not facing the considerable differences each of our histories brings to the present. Insisting "I don't see any differences" is disrespectful, Dwight Johnson reminds us.

If a black woman is upset and expresses herself passionately, she does not need to be told "Calm down!" cautions Dwight. Let her share her feelings, affirm her right to those feelings, and let her know you hear her.

In cross cultural, as in other workplace situations, the healthiest organizations and individuals are the ones who ask: "What can I learn?" Bob Sutton notes. Let go of defining situations as 'successes or failures.' Look to learn a new principle or affirm a constructive practice each time you face a challenge like what to do when your boss is the problem.

Again, the underlying task is to either address the problem directly and authentically with your boss or, if your boss cannot/will not have this mutually respectful conversation with you, make a choice: move on or stay on with clear boundaries.

One thing is certain: someone has to leave or change. If you were LaDonna, what would you choose?

A Personal Call

In the end, deciding what to do if your boss is the problem is a personal call. Only you can make that call. I hope that you, fortified by your own integrity and this information, feel better prepared to make that call if your boss is the problem. Remember:

"Above all, be the heroine of your life, not the victim."
Nora Ephron

Help for LaDonna

Meanwhile, LaDonna is about to walk into her "it's-time-to-get-everything-out-on-the-table" meeting with her boss, Marietta.

I'm interested: Has this article offered you any useful ideas? What in your own experience might help you coach LaDonna?

Each of us will have our own approach. Here's one possibility that flows from applying the steps above.

Prepare yourself: LaDonna needs to find out if Marietta is willing to let LaDonna lead the organization. If both LaDonna and Marietta stay on, both need clear job descriptions. If Marietta cannot let go of her need to control, that may be a deal-breaker for LaDonna.

Drop the attitude: LaDonna, now aware of Marietta's sabotage, accepts that she cannot change Marietta; however, she needs to set boundaries with Marietta on who will do what. LaDonna also needs to determine if Marietta's statements can be trusted. How will measurable expectations be set and assessed if an agreement can be forged?

Do damage control: LaDonna has worked on developing a trusting, straightforward relationship with James, and other Board members. They assure her she can stay on if she wants to and that they will deal with Marietta's inability to let go. LaDonna also begins work on her master's degree, seeking also to network her way into other possible jobs.

Set up the meeting and environment for success: With the Board's support, LaDonna invites Marietta to meet with her with the goal of establishing clear job descriptions and boundaries.

- **Agree on a time** when you can talk with each other without interruption: Friday morning works.

- **Set an agenda with time limitations:** Both agree that they will talk about who should be doing what.

- **If possible, meet in a neutral off-site location** like a quiet and private booth or table at a restaurant. Marietta suggests the local country club, where she is a member; LaDonna suggests a local restaurant, which has quiet and private booths.

- **Agree on the process you will use to resolve differences** including the 'we agree to disagree' option. Marietta tells LaDonna: "We don't have any differences. You just haven't been around long enough to understand how things work here." LaDonna suggests that James join them at the meeting to facilitate the conversation. Marietta, thinking James is 'in her pocket,' agrees.

Hold the meeting: LaDonna states that she needs full control over staff supervision; she will consult Marietta as needed. She then asks Marietta: "What do you need from me...?"

■ **Ask your boss: What do you need from me in order to work effectively together?** Marietta, offended, chides LaDonna saying: "Who do you think you are! You can't come in here and expect people to change. You have no idea how to direct a program. You've only been an Assistant Director; you have no experience."

■ **Discuss what changes each of you can and are willing to make:** Marietta says she isn't willing to make any changes. LaDonna says she needs to be free to supervise staff without being 'end run': Marietta smirks.

■ **Agree on next steps: If appropriate, end the meeting by stating one thing you honestly appreciate/value about the other person** — something you would miss if you no longer worked together. LaDonna tells Marietta: "You have done a remarkable job creating this program from scratch. I respect you for that. However, for me to stay on, I need to be able to do my job."

Assuming LaDonna is black and Marietta is white, what additional dynamics may need to be addressed in their relationship? Both women turn to James. What happens next? You decide.

References

Berg, C., Davis, M., Johnson, D., & Pritchett-Johnson, B. "Why do some white women struggle with managing black women?": Parts I and II. www.BAMradionetwork.com

Bruno, H. E. (2012). *What you need to lead: Emotional intelligence in practice.* Washington, DC: NAEYC.

Delong, T. J., Gabarro, J. J., & Lees, R. J. (2008, Summer). Why mentoring matters in a hypercompetitive world. *Journal of Applied Management Accounting Research*, 1-8.

Gabarro, J. "Leading the leader: Three rules for managing your boss." www.BAMradionetwork.com

Gabarro, J. J., & Kotter, J. P. (2005, January). Managing your boss. *Harvard Business Review*, 83(1).

Goleman, D. (2006). *Social intelligence: The new science of human relationships.* New York: Bantam Dell.

Snider, J. "Of bosses good and bad," *Hechinger Report.* http://hechingered.org/tags/jack-gabarro/

Sutton, R. "Good boss, bad boss: Which are you?" www.BAMradionetwork.com

Sutton, R. (2012). *Good boss, Bad boss: How to be the best... and learn from the worst.* New York: Grand Central Publishing.

Holly Elissa Bruno

Holly Elissa Bruno, MA, JD, is a best-selling author, international keynote speaker, ground-breaking radio host, and seasoned team builder. She served as Assistant Attorney General for the state of Maine and Assistant Dean at the University of Maine School of Law. An alumna of Harvard University's Institute for Educational Management, she teaches leadership courses for The McCormick Center for Early Childhood Leadership and Wheelock College. Holly Elissa's books include the best-selling, *What You Need to Lead an Early Childhood Program: Emotional Intelligence in Practice* (NAEYC, 2012), *Managing Legal Risks in Early Childhood Programs* (Columbia University's Teachers College Press, November 2012), and *Learning from the Bumps in the Road* (Redleaf Press, 2013). Her first book, *Leading on Purpose*, was published by McGraw-Hill in 2008. To share your story in Holly Elissa's upcoming book on 2nd chances, go to her blog at hollyelissabruno.com. To 'recovering attorney' Holly Elissa, life is too short to do anything but enjoy it daily.

3 CHAPTER 3
Managing the Organization

ECE and Business Savvy — A Happy Marriage *by Cecelia Doyle* 92

Are You Running a Center or Building an Organization?

by Joan Dunn Antonsen, Jan Silverman, and Pauline Work 95

Searching for Innovators: An Interview with Louise Stoney *by Margie Carter* 101

New Ways of Managing: Alternative Approaches to Leading

Early Childhood Organizations *by Roger Neugebauer*.......................................107

Becoming Community Centric *by Lisa Ann Haeseler* 110

Growing a Multi-site Organization: Build Systems of Credibility and

Empower Others to Execute Them *by Chad Dunkley* 114

Nine Questions for the Dedicated Board Member *by Roger Neugebauer*.......................117

Enjoying the Good Lice: Managing Crises *by Pauline Davey Zeece* 119

Considering Expansion? Lessons Learned Along the Way *by Henry Wilde*....................123

Out of the Box Ideas on Center Evaluation by *Roger Neugebauer*...........................128

Do You Have a Healthy Organization? *by Roger Neugebauer* 132

ECE and Business Savvy

A Happy Marriage

by Cecelia Doyle

*"There is nothing more difficult to take in hand,
more perilous to conduct,
or more uncertain in its success
than to take the lead in the introduction of a
new order of things."*

Niccolò Machiavelli

Embracing Analytics

The best programs in early childhood education will create a culture based on customer service, which brings together best practices in business and education. Today's groundbreaking programs require business — *not* as usual. While program staff will continue to thrive in a culture of trust and collaboration, there's a twist. Both teachers and directors must know and apply data analysis to the work they do. Why, you ask? These educators/analysts recognize the parent as both the child's first and most important teacher *and* as the program's most important customer. The parent-as-customer approach requires a different kind of thinking that is rooted in analytics.

What does it mean to be both an early childhood educator and an analytical thinker? It means acting like a business owner, regardless of position or role, and solving problems by moving beyond opinion and toward data. Simply put, data is information that helps us understand 'what's going on.' Through analysis, we bring meaning to the information and, most importantly, improve the decisions we make on behalf of the children and families in our care. Let's look at an example:

Jake, the preschool teacher, was concerned about the falling enrollment in his classroom. He considered himself a 'pretty good' teacher and couldn't put his finger on why this was happening. Jake resisted the urge to think, "Enrollment is not my problem!" Rather, he acknowledged some hurt feelings and, at the same time, was propelled to do things differently. Jake is an owner — he is both President and CEO of his classroom. He understands that the success of his classroom is connected to the overall success of the business ('the Center'). Jake began to look for information by gathering the data he had collected previously: there were parent evaluations and parent conferences. However, this time he approached the information differently. He put on his analyst hat and began to dig into the data by asking:

This new way of thinking requires stepping outside the belief that "I'm just a teacher in the preschool room" or "just a center director." It is about being 'all in' and embracing the role of educator-analyst. The future requires early childhood programs with educators/analysts at all levels that deliver superior parent service. These educators/analysts make decisions by combining what they know is best for children with data analysis. The result will be families that remain in the program, which ensures consistency for children and continuity in revenue that contributes to high-quality care and education.

In early childhood programs we are always looking for opportunities to serve parents and children better. We do this by building on our capacity for empathy and add analytics. What should an educator/analyst do to ensure that the scenario I shared does not happen again? Lead with data and analysis to inform decisions around service! We may include opinion and anecdote as well, but not as the sole sources of input for our decision making. This mindset creates the greatest value for parents — their return on investment — and demonstrates customer

- Are there themes that might help me identify why enrollment is declining?

- What is the impact of enrollment decline on the business overall?

- Is there other data that I'm missing that could help solve the problem?

- What are the different solutions that might help improve the situation?

- How might the change(s) I'm considering impact my classroom or the Center as a whole?

Consider the following scenario and how a program's educators/analysts might respond:

I was rushing into the center to pick up my three daughters, ages 9 months, 2½, and 4. It was winter — already dark, snowy, and cold outside — and I had a lot on my mind. I had to retrieve my girls from three different classrooms and do it before a late fee was charged. This involved getting them into their winter gear; not forgetting their special stuffed animals, daily reports and artwork; fielding their questions and excitement in seeing me; and signing them out, all while mentally preparing the night's meal in my head. Of course underlying all this was a concern about being perceived as a good parent by the center staff: someone who has it all together.

I remember this experience well because it did not go quite like that.

I picked up my infant daughter, then on to the toddler and preschool rooms. My toddler had other ideas, which will not surprise you if you have any experience with a two year old! I opened the classroom door and picked up my daughter's winter coat and special belongings. She took off down the hall and out of sight, discarding her coat along the way. I spent the next several minutes trying to locate her and then coax her to put on her coat (she never did). A teacher called out asking me to come back and sign out. I was at my wit's end just trying to manage three little girls, get to the car (oh yes, and get them into car seats!), and get home. Ultimately, I could either collect my toddler daughter or her coat. I chose the daughter and left her coat lying in the hallway.

service as a fundamental part of the organizational culture. Let's look at another example and see how the center director responded.

Conclusion

What if we hired only MBAs to run our classrooms full of three year olds? I have a better idea. As early childhood educators, what if we mastered business know-how and used it to inform how we serve parents in our programs?

We need business sense to run high-quality early childhood programs. 'Advocates' are educator/advocates who apply business know-how to make things better for children and families. These skilled professionals seize opportunities to marry best practices in early childhood education with business acumen. They grow leaders at all levels of the program and use data and analysis to drive decisions. This new skill set is revealing a new path into the future. Will you marry what you know is good for kids with business savvy? E-mail me one action you will take to become an edvocate. I will respond with a note of encouragement. We can do this!

Cecelia Doyle

Cecelia Doyle is the Academic Director for Early Childhood Education at Collegis Education. She previously led Rasmussen College's Early Childhood Education Programs as School Dean. Cece earned her doctorate in education from the College of Education and Human Development at the University of Minnesota and was selected as a member of the Minnesota Governor's Early Childhood Advisory Council, Professional Development Committee, and former Center Director.

Are You Running a Center or Building an Organization?

by Joan Dunn Antonsen, Jan Silverman, and Pauline Work

Years ago, centers serving 100 children were an anomaly. Today, not only are 100 child centers commonplace, but centers serving 200 and even 300 children in one location are no longer atypical.

Likewise, local, regional, and national child care chains have experienced unprecedented growth in this same decade. In short, this has been a period of dramatic change for child care centers — a period of dramatic growth.

When a 50-child center doubles its capacity in five years, or when a single center branches out to offer care in five different locations, more is changing than the number of children being served. In a period of expansion, relationships among individuals within the organization undergo dramatic, often wrenching changes. Similarly, the relationship of the organization to the community it serves changes — to the satisfaction of some segments in the community, and to the dissatisfaction of others. In the article that follows, the authors address the problems that occur when a center grows and changes, but the center's management does not.

The Case of the Indispensable Entrepreneur

Henrietta brimmed over with pride the day her baby, the Duck Duck Goose Day Care Center was highlighted on a local TV newscast as the "sterling example of how child care would work in a perfect world." Indeed, Duck Duck Goose was Henrietta's baby and, indeed, it was exemplary.

Henrietta got her start caring for six preschoolers in her home. As her reputation as a loving caregiver spread by word of mouth, Henrietta found it necessary to move the program out of her house, to rent increasingly larger storefronts and church basements, and to hire more and more teachers to supplement her efforts. Before long, Henrietta recognized her ultimate dream as she obtained financing to design and build her own facility.

What made this rapid expansion possible was not only Henrietta's loving attention to the children, but also her warm relations with the parents, her uncanny memory for details, and her seemingly endless capacity for hard work. Even though Henrietta now employed over 20 teachers, she still tried to spend a few hours every day in the classrooms to be with the children, to work with the newer teachers, and to maintain control of the center's curriculum. While the center now served over 100 families, Henrietta still remembered all the parents' names and shared in their joys and sorrows.

"The problems of managing a growing organization are not insurmountable, but they do become more severe as the rate of growth accelerates, and organizations that grow very rapidly are often managed so badly that they ultimately collapse."

Theodore Caplow, in *Managing an Organization*

Even though Duck Duck Goose now operated on a $400,000 budget, Henrietta still ran it by the seat of her pants. She kept items needing immediate attention on top of her desk, bills to pay in the top left drawer, receipts in the bottom left drawer, and payroll records in the bottom right drawer. What kept this shoebox accounting system from self-destructing was Henrietta's memory. She never forgot to deposit payroll taxes, never let a parent get behind in fees without a gentle reminder, always paid bills on time, and always remembered when a teacher was due an annual increase.

However, keeping Duck Duck Goose alive and well required a heroic effort on Henrietta's part. She was on the scene to handle every crisis, she seldom took a vacation, and she routinely put in 60-hour work weeks.

After carrying on like this for 20 years, and loving every moment of it, Henrietta decided she would like to retire from her job when her husband retired from his. She appointed the head teacher to take her place, and looked forward to a well-deserved life of leisure. Six months later, she was back working 60 hours a week at Duck Duck Goose, as her replacement was blown away by all the administrative details. Now Henrietta had to work harder than ever to straighten out the mess.

What Went Wrong

In a nutshell, what went wrong was that Henrietta was so busy running her center that she failed to build an organization that could run without her. Henrietta's case is, of course, fictional; but it is borrowed closely from real life. All too many directors, both of non profit and for profit centers, are so gung-ho about making their centers bigger and more profitable that they never get around to making them stronger and more adaptive. Here are some of the mistakes directors such as Henrietta make:

■ **The Wonder Woman Syndrome (also known as The One Man Band Syndrome).** This syndrome consists of one part egoism ("This is my center"), one part over-confidence ("I can do everything"), one part condescension ("If I want it done right, I'd better do it myself"), and one part masochism ("60-hour weeks — I love it"). Wonder Woman protects the center with her heroic efforts. She meets every crisis head on, she resolves every conflict, she makes every decision, she soothes every disgruntled parent, she unplugs every clogged toilet.

Being Wonder Woman is a demanding job, but it is not without its rewards. Feeling indispensable can be rewarding. Members of the organization can also provide lots of strokes for working so hard on behalf of the center. However, by doing everything herself, Wonder Woman fails to allow her staff to grow. Never given full responsibility for anything important, staff members fail to develop any administrative skills. Never allowed to make decisions or to think for themselves, staff members fail to develop any sense of responsibility.

■ **The Bigger is Better Syndrome.** If a director succeeds in expanding a one-room child care center into a system providing care in five locations, that magnitude of achievement can be a heady experience. This sense of progress can easily obscure deterioration in quality of services.

In a center's headlong effort to expand, hiring and training standards may be relaxed, the spontaneity and creativity of the staff may be lost, and communication with parents may become more cold and businesslike. The very qualities that gave the center a strong reputation in the community and enabled it to grow in the first place may be disregarded as the center attempts to capitalize on its reputation, thus sowing the seeds for the organization's eventual decline.

■ **The Stegosaurus Syndrome.** Dinosaurs were the peak performers of their era; but when conditions changed, they fell on hard times. Likewise, many directors excel in a particular environment but fail to keep pace when the ground rules change. This failure to adapt to changing conditions is the result of a critical shortsightedness. For example, a typical Stegosaurus director was extremely effective at attracting public monies to his center in the 1970s. He was a prolific proposal writer, an artful negotiator, an efficient administrator of government contracts, and a skillful report writer. Yet, when government funding started to dry up, he was not able to look ahead and identify other funding sources to nurture, other markets to explore. As a result, his center gradually went under.

"To stay on the upward growth curve requires a broadening of the management talent base — some effective staffing that adds up to a well rounded functional team.... The manager must begin getting results through others."
Steven C. Brandt in *Enterpreneuring*

Building an Organization

The difference between a director who is running a center and one who is building an organization has been summarized as the difference between being an administrator and being a manager. An administrator is a very good technician — he can capably carry out all the day-to-day tasks involved in operating the center. But his focus is narrowly on the here and now

— "What do I need to do to keep the center afloat this week?"

The manager's focus, on the other hand, is always two steps ahead. She is able to look beyond the day-to-day details and see the broader picture. She is attuned to shortcomings in the daily performance of the center, to current opportunities for the center to make an impact, and to future trends that may affect the center.

So, assuming that you aspire to be a manager and to build your organization, where do you start? Listed are four not-so-simple tasks to get you well on your way:

**Task 1:
Building a Managerial Team.**

Henrietta made herself indispensable — Duck Duck Goose couldn't run without her. The goal of an aspiring manager should be to make herself completely dispensable. You should strive to surround yourself with people who take over major portions of your job. Building this managerial team involves three separate steps:

■ **Analyze your workload.** Make a list of all your jobs — those that you spend most of your time on, as well as those you believe you should be doing but never seem to find the time for. Now organize them into functional categories. Theodore Caplow suggests, for example, that in a growing organization there are at least three managerial jobs that need to be done: running the existing organization, supervising the expansion, and coping with the unpredictable problems that expansion creates. On the other hand, you may chose to divide your responsibilities along more conventional, functional lines, i.e., financial management, staff supervision, planning, marketing.

Finally, study your categories and see how many of them you could give away. Identify those functions that someone else could do as well as you could, if not better, and those that would be the best invest-ment of your time.

■ **Identify potential team members.** Obvious-ly not everyone on your staff, nor everyone you could recruit off the street, is capable of perform-ing at a managerial level. In building a managerial team, you need to find people who are capable of functioning on their own, who are willing to take risks and make difficult decisions, and who are eager to grow. Just as importantly, they should share your vision of where the organization should be headed, and they should be people you are comfortable working with closely on a day-to-day basis.

You should make every effort to seek out manage-rial talent within your own organization. Before making a long-term commitment to someone who you believe has managerial potential, test her out by upping her routine responsibilities, or by giving her a challenging one-shot assignment.

■ **Delegate.** The only way to develop your manage-rial team is on-the-job training. If you cling to your Wonder Woman habits, you will prevent anyone else from sharing your load, or ultimately taking over for you.

Delegating is a painful, risky process. To help make it work, and to prevent disasters resulting from premature overload, you should release responsibility gradually. Start by assigning routine parts of a function, such as the bookkeeping task of the financial management function. Explain the task very carefully, and be readily available for questions and suggestions. Then assign the budding manager moderately difficult and clearly defined problems to solve (Which health insur-ance plan should we go with? How can we sched-ule staff in the afternoon?), and ask her to bring the options to you for a final decision. Once a team member has demonstrated ability at these lower levels, it is time to turn over a larger piece of the action to her and ask that she periodically keep you informed about what she is doing and what decisions she has made. Finally, you can turn over the full responsibility for a function and say, "You're on your own, don't bother me."

The first stages of delegation can require a lot of time, patience, and tolerance. However, when you get to the final stage, when you have groomed someone so well that you can rely on her totally, the amount of support this provides to you makes the entire effort worthwhile. The easiest way to sabotage the delegation process is to allow end runs. Let's say, for example, you have delegated fee collection to a head teacher, and one of the parents comes to you asking for more time to pay her overdue fees. The easy thing for you to do would be to make a decision on the spot like you always used to do. However, this would undermine the authority of the head teacher in the eyes of the parents, and demonstrate to the head teacher that you aren't really taking the delegation seriously. As a rule, once you delegate, don't vacillate.

Task 2:
Building an Administrative System.

One sure way to add stability to a program in the process of change is to avoid making the same decisions over and over again. Formal policies and procedures should be worked out for dealing with common problems and questions.

Procedures should be worked out, put in writing, and distributed to all staff for handling typical problems, such as a child becoming sick at the center, a teacher calling in sick at the last moment, a bus breaking down on a field trip, a fire breaking out in the center, or a furnace going out in midday. Likewise, regular schedules and flow charts should be worked out for routine functions. For example, it should be decided who gets what financial reports on what days, or who handles inquiries from parents checking out the school, and how such inquiries are handled.

The routinizing of administrative functions does smack of bureaucratic red tape. Certainly if procedures become too rigid, they can take the life out of an organization. But given a healthy dose of common sense, committing routine procedures to paper does add a degree of stability that is important in an organization undergoing change. The center shouldn't be thrown into an uproar every time a problem arises and the director is not there to deal with it. Working out administrative systems also saves a lot of time and energy that is otherwise wasted on continually reinventing the wheel.

Task 3:
Tuning In to One's Environment.

Increasingly, child care centers are at the mercy of forces beyond their control. A decision in Washington, DC, to up the production of Stealth bombers may cause child care subsidies to be slashed. An inflammatory article in the local paper about a child care scandal clear across the country may add to a center's enrollment woes. A shift in the local employment structure may wreck havoc with a center's traditional customer base.

Directors who are not alert to such events and trends may allow their centers to be jeopardized by an unexpected threat, or to miss out on a new opportunity. Therefore, a director who desires to build a strong organization needs to tune in to what's happening outside the center as much as what's happening within the organization. The following are some means of keeping informed:

■ **Keeping in close contact with the parents.**
As an organization grows, it is very easy for the director to become increasingly isolated from the parents the center serves. It is critical to counteract this by structuring into one's work week some time to talk to parents, to keep in touch with their current needs and concerns.

■ **Tracking changing needs in the community by maintaining records of phone inquiries.**
Data on needs and means of those currently in the marketplace is an excellent barometer of changing local needs.

■ **Watching your center's financial trends.**
Knowing where you've been, what programs are making money, what programs are losing money, are strong indicators of where you should be heading.

■ **Volunteering to speak to local employer and parent groups.** The questions you are confronted with in these sessions will keep you in touch with community concerns about child care.

■ **Participating in a directors' group.** Comparing notes with other directors will allow you to check out your hunches about trends and changes.

■ **Discussions in staff meetings and board meetings about people's perceptions about community needs and developments increase the numbers of eyes and ears you have working for you.**

"Adaptive managers must adapt swiftly to immediate pressures — yet think in terms of long-range goals. Above all, the adaptive manager today must be capable of radical action — willing to think beyond the thinkable: to reconceptualize products, procedures, programs, and purposes before crisis makes drastic change inescapable."

Alvin Tofler, in *The Adaptive Corporation*

Task 4:
Maintaining a Long-range View.

To be effective in building an organization, you need to have some idea of what you are building toward. What do you want your center to look like in five years? Who will it be serving? What services will it provide? What needs to happen to realize this vision? To develop long-range action plans:

■ **Do plenty of 'what if' planning.** With your staff or board, do some brainstorming about potential scenarios and possible plans. Ask, "What if we... opened a new center in the suburbs?... offered a computer camp?... doubled our fees?" Explore the best/worst outcomes for each scenario.

■ **Establish some long-range goals.** Spell out what you would like your center to be doing in five years and what you want it to look like. Then outline a plan of action — lay out what needs to happen during those five years to move your center from point A to point B.

■ **Take some risks.** Seldom will a plan of action come with a guarantee of success. If your center is to keep pace with changing needs, you will need to act at times when you can't be sure of what will happen. In those cases, you will have to trust your own judgment and be willing to make some mistakes. When you shrink from taking risks, you stop growing. Conversely, the more risks you take, the more you accelerate your learning, and the better you get at making judgment calls.

■ **Never give up.** As you try out new ideas to meet changing needs in the community, you have to expect that some of them will succeed, that some of them will fail, and that none of them will succeed forever. If you are content with running a center, you will continue to plug away at accustomed ways of doing business. However, if you want to build an organization with a future, you need to be continually open to new ideas and new directions.

Joan Dunn Antonsen

Joan Dunn Antonsen was executive director of the Fruit and Flower Child Care Center in Portland, Oregon.

Jan Silverman

Jan Silverman was director of Lucky Lane Early Childhood Association in St. Louis, Missouri.

Pauline Work

Pauline Work was director of Child Care Services for the YWCA of Metropolitan Chicago, in Chicago, Illinois.

Searching for Innovators

An Interview with Louise Stoney

by Margie Carter

I'm continually searching for innovative people in our field who are 'in the thick of it' trying to expand current notions of quality beyond a focus on regulations and rating scales. I look in the trenches for those working directly with children or managing an early childhood program; I seek out folks in big systems who aren't trapped in bureaucratic thinking; and I talk to teacher educators working in a variety of settings such as community colleges, training organizations, or independent consulting services. It fills me with hope, discovering folks who are piloting new possibilities and challenging us to move beyond the limits of our current thinking. I'd like to spotlight some of these voices for *Exchange* readers by sharing some of the dialogs we've been having.

Innovator: Louise Stoney, Alliance for Early Childhood Finance

As the co-founder of the Alliance for Early Childhood Finance, Louise Stoney is immersed in finding creative new finance and business strategies for our field. Her Exchange article "Shared Services: A powerful strategy to support sustainability of ECE Businesses" (Stoney, 2009) is an important read and offers a window into not only the value of shared services, but also a look at how an innovative mind works. My thinking has greatly benefited from our dialog.

Margie: Louise, I immediately resonated with your statement, "State ECE leaders have begun to craft industry-wide standards (such as professional development systems and quality rating systems), but the ECE industry has yet to create the infrastructure and supports individual programs and providers need to not only comply with these standards but to operate efficiently." This is a point I have been trying to make in my writing and consultation work. In my Exchange article "Assessing quality: What are we doing? Where are we going?" I tried to name this elephant in the room. The early childhood field seems to think that implementing more standards and rating scales will improve quality and outcomes for children. Rarely do you hear the idea that to sustain quality, teachers must be provided with more off-the-floor time to plan and to talk through the complex tasks of understanding the teaching and learning process. My question is this: Without such provisions, how can we genuinely professionalize our field so as to attract, retain, and support reflective teachers who understand the *Why* behind any standard and seek to translate theory into practice?

Louise: You are right. I think it's important to acknowledge that accountability to standards and implementing effective practice are different things; people often speak the words standards and results in the same breath, but it's a very complex dance. Yes, we need standards; they provide an essential framework for the field and define — in very general ways — the inputs that help produce results and the costs associated with those inputs. Documents, checklists, and rating systems are ways to ensure standards are met, so I understand they are needed. But supporting early learning is far more complex.

Margie: And isn't supporting early learning what everyone says they are concerned about these days? How do we link that idea with an expanded notion of quality? My experience in assessing quality leads me to look more closely at an organization's budget and program infrastructure to see if they have established a foundation for quality improvement beyond a score on a rating scale at any given moment. I look for evidence that teachers and directors have the time and motivation to maintain a focus on self-assessment, reflective practice, and continuous improvement in early learning experiences for children. In reading about the Alliance for Early Childhood Finance, I see your work as trying to help individual programs take a careful look at more sustainable fiscal systems, but you are also trying to tackle the larger systemic issues of financing a viable ECE system. We just don't hear enough from folks trying to tackle this.

Louise: Isn't it interesting that our experiences, which are totally different — you working with teachers and directors, me working with finance and policymakers — lead us to the same place?

Margie: I'm incredibly drawn to Shared Services as a solution to addressing quality through more viable business practices, but I think finances are only one part of the administrative equation for quality. Would you agree that in early childhood settings we are so accustomed to living within our meager means that we've downsized our thinking about quality?

Louise: That's what I mean about arriving at the same place. I think your emphasis on supporting

teachers is just right, and it's a key outcome that I'd like to see from the shared services' work. Until recently the shared services 'movement' was largely focused on the financial bottom line — because along with support, teachers need better wages, access to health and retirement benefits, and so forth. And garnering the resources to pump into staff means streamlining the funding we spend on administration. Yes, you can raise more money. But only up to a point; you've really got to be wise in how you spend that money. There is no margin for error in an ECE budget. You've got to shave every cost you can, and smart administration is where I think we can find those cost savings. Often, I see centers that appear to be fiscally stable and have a well-compensated director but you still see classroom staff with lousy wages and little or no benefits.

Margie: Amen, sister!

Louise: Another big part of the problem is what I call the 'Iron Triangle' of ECE finance (Stoney & Mitchell, 2011). The three points on this triangle are full enrollment, full fee collection, and having rates that cover your costs (or raising third party funding to fill the gap). Everyone focuses on the third leg — the rate — but to remain fiscally viable an ECE program has to stay full and collect every dollar that is owed. And achieving this goal isn't easy. You've got to stay on top of it all the time and you've got to fill out the paperwork correctly and on time, apply for every grant you possibly can. Basically, an ECE program really needs a sophisticated fiscal office, which is way too expensive for a small, independent, stand-alone center.

Margie: So here is that quality dilemma again. Programs need sophisticated business practices but also an administrator with people skills, pedagogical understandings, and the wherewithal to develop an organizational culture that reflects his or her values on how to achieve quality.

Louise: The more I worked on ECE finance the more I felt that the field was setting directors up to fail. It is such a complex job and ECE directors work so hard, but they just can't do everything well. It's not humanly possible. So the tendency is to focus on what you can do, what gives you energy, and just hope that the other pieces fall into place. We all avoid doing what we don't do well; it's a survival strategy. I think that's what happens with fiscal management in ECE; directors avoid the problem or reach for simple solutions like continually pushing on public reimbursement rates. Many directors just don't want to look at business management as part of the solution because it shines a light on what they don't do well. But if you can't shine a light on it — and diagnose the problem — then you can't intervene. So I keep trying to come up with ways to help directors feel more comfortable about not being good at everything. I would like them to see that being clear about what they don't like doing and don't do well, and figuring out a way to partner with someone else to do that piece of the work is a sign of profound strength rather than an admission of weakness.

Restructuring to Take Quality to a New Level

Margie: You are reminding me of the remarkable process London Bridge Child Care Services in London, Ontario, Canada went through some years ago when they came to a similar realization. Their goal was to take quality to a new level, and they started by centralizing administration across their 14 centres. They assumed this would just naturally free up time for the directors to focus on new quality and curriculum practice. But they learned this wasn't enough. To transform themselves they needed to do two additional things:

■ Design a strong leadership development program (which turned out to
be an 18-month-long effort, with
inspiration drawn from business,
philosophy, art, and child development
theory)

■ Work with their centre directors to assess what they were skilled at and what they really enjoyed

and then begin to redefine their roles and responsibilities.

Some went into the central office to focus on the administrative duties, while others stayed in centres with different responsibilities, focusing on the people in the program, supporting families, mentoring teachers in their ongoing development, and shifting the learning culture of their centre. I encourage anyone who wants to see what shared services and an expanded vision of quality can accomplish to consider participating in a study tour to London Bridge!

Business and Pedagogical Expertise

Louise: I don't think I could have engaged in this dialogue 10 years ago. Back then I was still convinced the answer was more money. It wasn't until many years of successful work on ECE finance that I realized the problem was more complex. After watching all my good work have so little impact with the small, community-based programs I cared about so much (sometimes it felt like pouring water into a sieve), it dawned on me that if we didn't focus on strengthening the ECE industry as a whole, we were going to continue to waste our precious resources — human and fiscal. That was the dawn of the shared services work. But I, too, have learned that change is a multi-faceted process. And you just named a key component, which I think you call pedagogical leadership, right?

Margie: Yes. Part of the equation is getting more business-savvy administrative practices in programs, but equally important is getting more pedagogical expertise in the leadership so that someone is keeping the organizational culture focused on the teaching process among the children, staff, and families. This is because we are not only an industry, but a profession focused on teaching and learning. You talked earlier about the iron triangle of ECE finance. In addition to this triangle we need an intersecting one that focuses on our professional endeavors, on the people in the program, not only supervising to ensure they are in compliance with standards, but

---

How Shared Services Improve Quality

- Assures professional fiscal management

- Offers the economic strength of a larger organization so very small businesses can weather economic ebbs and flows.

- Provides more career opportunities and better working conditions, wages, and benefits for staff.

- Creates opportunities for pedagogical leadership, including teacher mentors, coaches, communities of practice, and focused time for staff to reflect and plan.

- Lowers costs from economies of scale in business functions like payroll, banking, janitorial, benefits management, and services.

For more information visit:
www.opportunities-exchange.org

---

mentoring the teachers in their own learning, and creating an organizational culture that partners with the children's families. In our book, *The Visionary Director* (Carter & Curtis, 2010), Deb Curtis and I describe this as a tri-angle framework for directing a program that brings your vision to life. We urge people to think of quality in this expanded way. I'm wondering how your thinking is moving forward when it comes to the role shared services can play in expanding thinking and actual practices related to quality.

Louise: I think that the work you are doing is the next frontier for the shared services movement. Reflective practice is key to early learning and — as you point out — it requires time, leadership, and

discipline. You have identified several important steps in that reflective process: a focus on observing children; creating an organizational culture that encourages and supports observation; establishing protocols teachers can use to analyze their observations and use them to guide practice; involving teachers in communities of practice so they can share ideas and learn from one another; and strong pedagogical leadership, that makes time for reflective practice and facilitates the process until it becomes second nature. I don't know how an ECE director can possibly engage in that important work when they are the only leader in a center and responsible for everything. But if centers come together and share leadership and create new business models and management structures, they can free up time as well as administrative funds that can be shifted into expanding program quality. They can re-structure leadership roles to ensure fiscal sustainability and more significant pedagogical leadership.

How Pedagogical Leadership Improves Quality

- Keeps organizational culture focused on strengthening relationships and being a community.

- Provides resources, time, and protocols for teachers to meet and engage in professional development.

- Questions, provokes, and encourages teachers to learn alongside children.

- Engages families in the learning community, while someone else collects fees.

For more information visit:
www.ecetrainers.com

Margie: Shared services also offers promise with regard to bridging the divides we experience across race, culture, and class in our communities. For example, Sound Child Care Solutions (SCCS) (a Shared Service Alliance in Seattle, Washington) has expanded the idea of quality to include this goal.

Currently six centers located in diverse neighborhoods throughout the city — large and small, faith-sponsored and employer-sponsored, low-income and middle-class — are members of SCCS and see themselves as part of one organization, each center having its own unique identity. Their alliance allows all centers to tap multiple public and private funding streams which would not otherwise be possible at the individual sites, and the economies of scale provide stability as well as some cost efficiencies. Furthermore, SCCS takes pedagogical leadership seriously. A mentor teacher is now available to

all staff who now have opportunities for coursework and professional development, and can apply to participate in a monthly community of practice across centers to develop their leadership in pedagogical guidance for their program.

Moving in a New Direction

In challenging and uncertain economic times like the present, many people and organizations are reluctant to step outside of what is familiar and most common. In my mind, these times present us with an opportunity for innovation that could take us beyond anything we have yet imagined as possible for high-quality early childhood programming. Innovation sometimes involves bold, radical steps and in other cases, plotting a course with incremental steps that lead to new realities. As Jim Rohn said, "When

---

Growing Pedagogical Leadership at Sound Child Care Solutions

While all staff have personal mentors, they can also apply to join our 'pedagogical leaders project.' Those who participate get release time to meet monthly to consider new possibilities for simple materials such as playdough, buttons, and cups.

- We play because it re-connects us to the joy of learning through play.

- In playing we discover that the way we offer children materials can encourage or discourage sustained interest and ways to meet our learning goals.

- We uncover things to consider in our planning, documentation, and assessment process. We identify vocabulary to use with the children.

- We practice detailed observations in order to see children's lively minds, to honor children's interests, and also to identify learning outcomes that can be entered in CC-Net.

- We learn ways to put our observations and documentation into 'reference books' for the children so they can see themselves as thinkers, revisit vocabulary, and learn from each other's ideas.

- We practice writing learning stories from our observations and teachers' thinking about each event and invite a dialogue with the children's families and other teachers.

- We explore how to provide expanded leadership in our centers.

you know what you want, and want it badly enough,
you will find a way to get it. You cannot change your
destination overnight, but you can change your
direction overnight."

References

Carter, M. (2010, July/August). "Drive-through training."
Exchange, 194, 61-63.

Carter, M. (2008, November/December). "Assessing quality:
What are we doing? Where are we going?" *Exchange, 184*, 32-35.

Carter, M., & Curtis, D. (2010). *The visionary director: Organizing and improvising in your program* (2nd edition). St. Paul, MN:
Redleaf Press.

Stoney, L. (2009, September/October). "Shared services: A
powerful strategy to support sustainability of ECE businesses."
Exchange, 189, 68-71.

Stoney, L. (2011). The iron triangle: A simple formula for financial policy in ECE programs. [Online] www.earlychildhood
finance.org/downloads/.../IronTriangle_10.2010.pdf

Resources

London Bridge Child Care Services:
www.londonbridge.com

Sound Child Care Solutions:
www.soundchildcare.org

Opportunities Exchange:
www.opportunities-exchange.org

Margie Carter and Louise Stoney

Margie Carter and Louise Stoney have a fierce passion to see
early childhood program directors move out of isolation,
discover their best skills, and work in leadership teams to achieve
an expanded definition of quality and a work life that feels not
only possible, but rewarding. Find out more about Margie's work
at www.ecetrainers.com and Louise's work at
www.earlychildhoodfinance.org.

New Ways of Managing

Alternative Approaches to Leading

Early Childhood Organizations

by Roger Neugebauer

Thirty-eight years ago when *Exchange* was launched, the few textbooks on child care administration that existed described a standard management approach where a board of directors oversaw a single director of a single center. Of course, even at that time this model did not describe well the entire field — multi-site for profit organizations were being created around the country with regional management structures; 'mom and pop' centers were also on the rise where a husband and wife shared responsibilities; and parent co-ops were not uncommon.

Today, the range of approaches to managing early childhood organizations has become even more diverse. In this article I will give a few examples of these evolving structures. Then in 38 more years, I will take a new look.

Co-directing

Of course co-directing is not exactly new. As noted above, 38 years ago husbands and wives collaborated on operating a significant share of centers. Typically one spouse would be responsible for curriculum issues and the other administrative responsibilities. Over the years, the idea that it takes two has found new variations.

Most often two individuals work together as co-directors — one again focusing on pedagogical matters and the other on administrative responsibilities. The point noted in the introduction to this book was that a director needs "14 hands" to handle the diverse range of tasks to run a center. Well, with two directors, each one only needs 7 hands; it's still a lot of work, but much more realistic.

A year ago the director of Our Redeemer's Preschool in Helena, Montana, retired. The teachers met and decided to propose having two of them serve as co-directors. They approached the church about the concept, and while there was some resistance to this 'radical' model, it was approved. Today, Trudy Burke works in the morning and is primarily responsible for financial matters. Mary Robertson works in the afternoon and is primarily responsible for parent relations. All teachers work together to plan and deliver the curriculum. Burke and Robertson each work 30 hours a week, spending 50% of their time in the classroom and 50% on administrative matters.

Shared Services

Shared services is a concept that has gained a lot of momentum in the past decade; there are now even annual shared services conferences. The concept encompasses a diverse range of centers working together to economically provide top-notch administrative services. At the outset, the way this worked was that a group of centers in a community would cooperate as follows: the center that had the strongest financial management person would take over those services for all the centers, one with strength in the marketing area would take that on, and so on.

Sound Child Care Solutions (SCCS) has taken this model a step farther. This consortium was inspired by the recognition that small child care centers, for profit and non profit alike, operate in a 'chronic state of financial fragility.' SCCS provides centralized consortium staff whose costs are shared by all participating centers. SCCS staff provide financial, payroll, and benefits management. In addition, they provide grant writing, past due bill collection, handling of public subsidy paperwork, wait list management, and human resource technical assistance. And, as the consortium has evolved, it now provides pedagogical support such as coordinated professional development, mentoring, assessment, and staff recruitment.

Each center in the consortium retains its independence and maintains its cultural identity. Each center still has a director who makes final enrollment decisions, oversees daily programming and curriculum planning, and retains all hiring and firing authority.

Contracted Management

The Chambliss Center for Children is not a new program. It was founded in 1872 when a group of local church women started an orphanage that later became known as the Vine Street Orphans Home. In 1986, the United Way asked Chambliss to take over the operation of a struggling child care center at Howard High School. Over the following years, Chambliss took over the management of five more community-based child care centers and 10 school-based programs. Today, Chambliss serves more than 300 children in its Extended Child Care program ('24/7/365'), in addition to managing other community programs, operating a residential program for

children who have been removed from their homes by the courts, manages 15 foster homes, and collaborates with Head Start in 21 shared classrooms.

Only one of the community-based sites has a full-time, on-site director. Management in the remaining sites is provide by staff hired by Chambliss who work as a team and divide their time among the sites. Each program has a manager on-site at least half-time. One (or more) lead teacher at each site is the designated 'go-to' person in the event that management staff is not on-site.

Each of the independent sites has its own board of directors, which negotiates a management contract with Chambliss. The Treasurer and Board for each site work with Chambliss to develop the annual budget. Chambliss manages all administrative, fiscal, payroll, insurance, maintenance, and food purchasing services. All programs are expected to participate in the Tennessee Star Quality Rating System.

Über Outsourcing

For decades many early childhood programs have engaged in outsourcing of janitorial, transportation, and payroll services. Recently the David and Laura Merage Foundation took this concept and super-sized it in the Early Learning Ventures (ELV) initiative, which today serves more than 600 child care providers and impacts over 40,000 children in Colorado.

Centers that elect to join ELV have access to a wide range of administrative tools including bulk purchasing, streamlined communication with regulatory and funding agencies, and fiscal services. They can elect to participate in any one of four 'tiers' of services. The list of services includes:

■ enrollment.

■ registration and wait list.

■ staff demographics.

- certification and training.

- child attendance.

- staff-child ratios.

- billing.

- child development tracking.

ELV is looking to extend the advantages of its model. It recently was awarded an Early Head Start – Child Care Partnership grant to serve more than 240 Colorado children and families. A second opportunity that ELV is exploring is Pay for Success, or the Social Impact Bond Initiative. A Pay for Success Bond is a contract with the public sector in which a commitment is made to pay for improved social outcomes that result in public sector savings. ELV hopes to support the growth and quality enhancement of its members by acting as the fiscal sponsor for Pay for Success models in the early childhood sector.

Franchising

In the late 1960s when for profit child care organizations were exploding on the scene, most of them started using the basic franchising model. However, within a decade, most organizations had abandoned the franchise model in favor of a company-owned approach. They discovered that maintaining quality control in far-flung programs was impossible — you could not maintain control by sending out cases of buns, burgers, and uniforms with instructions on how hot and how long to cook the products. Nor could you control the quality of the programs by sending out reams of paper with curriculum ideas.

However, once Al Gore invented the Internet, it became feasible to both support and monitor the quality of franchised centers more effectively and efficiently. As a result, franchising child care organizations are currently the fastest growing sector in the U.S. child care sector.

A child care 'franchisor' licenses its trademarks and proven business methods to others (often husband

and wife teams) in exchange for a recurring payment, a percentage of gross sales, or a fixed fee.

For a franchisee to succeed in the child care business, it must receive significant ongoing support from the franchisor. For example, Primrose Schools, one of the longest-standing child care franchisors, provides its clients with specifications on center designs and equipment, extensive in-person and interactive training support, a 'robust research-informed' curriculum, student and teacher assessment tools, and uniform branding and marketing materials. In addition, it conducts a national marketing campaign to drive awareness of the Primrose brand and provides parent communication resources to continue the home-to-school connection.

For a franchisor to succeed, the quality of services provided by franchisees must be maintained at a high level. Primrose maintains quality control by monitoring compliance on an ongoing basis and by providing continuous learning opportunities for franchisees.

A Final Word

The purpose of this article was not to provide an in-depth exploration of each of these models. Nor does it pretend to be comprehensive in covering all 'new ways of managing.' There are certainly many other innovative models out there such as staff cooperatives, employer supported operations, team-based management, and programs without walls. What I hoped to do is to stimulate emerging and mature leaders in our field to think out of the box when it comes to structures for providing high-quality services for all families, rich and poor, in a contemporary, cost-effective manner.

Roger Neugebauer

Roger Neugebauer is publisher of *Exchange Magazine* and a co-founder of the World Forum Foundation.

Becoming Community Centric

by Lisa Ann Haeseler

To be competent in their role, early educators must be knowledgeable and compassionately aware of local community resources. This includes connecting with neighborhood resources and appropriately matching programs to families' needs. These local resources include shelters, soup kitchens, rescue animal agencies, and emergency medical organizations.

Learning about other agencies in the community can be rewarding and a lot of fun. Collaboratively and collectively, many innovative ideas can arise from building upon these interdisciplinary, interagency partnerships, a vital component to organizational development. Just think about how much better you can serve children and families! Consider stepping out of your usual mode of mandatory workshops and inspire staff to enjoy themselves while learning and growing with their neighborhood colleagues. This kind of enlightened professional development is neighborhood-friendly and connects community professionals dedicated to serving young children and families. You send a clear, positive message to families, as well as to your local community, that you and your staff fully support the community and want to capitalize on its resources to help the neighborhood. This kind of leadership inspires everyone.

Neighborhood-driven initiatives call for creativity, cooperation, problem-solving, critical thinking, and a commitment to ongoing communication. Here's one way you might launch such an initiative in your program:

> Good morning! We are embarking on an exciting new initiative to build partnerships with resources in our neighborhood. We'll be learning who our community colleagues are, what they do to serve our community, and perhaps most importantly, how we as ECE professionals, can help them serve our children and families. Let's brainstorm, with partners and in small groups first, and then as a whole team, about how to locate the many resources (people and places) in our local area.

After about ten minutes, come back together as a whole team to record small groups' responses on chart paper. Next, ask staff to generate ideas for how to invite local organizations to share their resources with you, as well as to plan visits to community organizations to learn how you can partner with them. Some of the resources organizations typically need include clothing, money, and food donations; books; food pantry volunteers; and help with local

Red Cross, Salvation Army, and/or United Way drives.

As director, ensure that making these connections across agencies is fun for everyone involved. This work can transform your agency and your staff. Engage your staff in understanding at a deeper level the ecological (or life space) issues the families in your local community face on a daily basis. Collectively, critically evaluate the programs, events, and service delivery methods that children and families require.

Identifying Existing Community Resources: Broad-based Strategies

■ Have staff serve as fact finders for aid to families. Some families may not even be aware that they need help or that appropriate, low-cost services are available to them locally. These may include behavioral, social, and academic; family abuse; parenting and discipline; family safety and nutrition.

■ Consider levels of urgency of family needs. Begin your mission of community involvement by assisting families that require the most help, such as those experiencing trauma, turmoil, or abuse.

■ Locate and partner with local community services personnel such as child welfare workers, social service providers, and law enforcement personnel. Invite them to your agency to describe the services they offer, and of most importance, how you can work together to serve families more effectively. Ask if you can attend their meetings to continue learning about their services. Often law enforcement organizations offer workshops surrounding familial safety concerns and warning signs of which ECE staff should be aware.

■ Partner with local vocational schools and colleges, particularly their social work and community studies program departments. Learn from professors who publish research in the area of child development and others who develop the resourc-

es that families need to be successful. Consider mentoring college students who are studying early childhood education. This is a win-win situation: a student obtains classroom work experience and staff showcases their program, training the future workforce.

■ Expand community learning and giving efforts to include the children's family members and local community members. For example, invite community members to learn along with you and your staff about healthy eating tips, healthy recreation, safety indoors and outdoors, and ways to build habits for good health. Include recreation directors, park rangers, and wildlife animal rescue providers. Visit these professionals on field trips that include family members. Expand your community outreach to include before- and after-school agencies, community centers, and youth groups, including faith-based organizations.

■ Remind your staff that being a professional includes fun! Take field trips to senior citizen community/retirement homes to share smiles and laughter. Encourage children to create thank-you cards. Combining community service dedication, literacy skills, and a sense of civic-mindedness in children at a young age instills these values in children and helps them feel a sense of ownership in helping to make the neighborhood better and safer. Expand the writing of thank-you cards to include community helpers, such as Officer Bob and his canine companion, CC. Kids love dogs — and many other animals. Showing them how to care for animals helps them develop important life skills. Children will be eager to show off their 'Community Member' tag or hat, made with paste and love.

Search Strategies

Consider the following ideas for identifying and organizing community resources:

■ Begin by identifying all of the needs of your enrolled families: tutoring, food, transportation, housing, parenting classes, mental health services, financial guidance, and so on.

■ List the services your program or organization currently offers to families.

■ Contact your local mental health, medical health, and family clinics to identify their level of outreach and the full range of services they offer. (Remember, families' needs are often multifaceted and can require a great deal of coordination of services.)

■ Search the records of your local chamber of commerce to locate agencies offering low-cost and sliding-scale fees for services.

■ Contact other service agencies in your community, such as your local public health department and department of social services to learn about other neighborhood resources available to families.

■ Include private sector services in your search. While possibly more costly, professionals working in the private sector can assist you in navigating the bureaucracy and paperwork of medical insurance, for example, and may provide some low-cost services.

■ Visit hospitals, mental health, and family counseling clinics to collect their brochures, pamphlets, and business cards.

■ Ask everyone you visit, "Who do you know who helps families with _____?"

■ Enlist the aid of local agencies that provide emergency services to families. They often maintain directories of local services that assist families.

■ Start your own community service directory that includes websites, phone numbers, e-mails, and business cards. Organize these by service for easy retrieval.

Celebrate your staff's commitment to coming together to brainstorm, discuss, and collaborate on neighborhood initiatives to give back. Consider the follow-up meeting (adjacent box) where staff

demonstrate their new community-centric service mentality.

The director enters the room pushing a delicious cart of breakfast treats. She knows her staff has thought

---

"Good morning! I am very excited to hear your reports about your community spirit!"

Becky and Vicky begin by sharing how many of the families in their toddler room are headed by a single parent and that resources designed to meet their needs are hard to find. They tell how they created partnerships with a number of local free, low-cost, or sliding-scale family medical and mental health clinics; low-cost child care agencies; transitional and low-income housing units; and food banks and soup kitchens. And they are now each volunteering with one of these agencies once a month.

Next, Tanya and Jen had their own unique idea for giving back. Since their husbands are both mechanics, they offered free oil changes for mechanic shop clients who are also enrolled families.

Bill, Tony, and Jimmy report that they are going to collaborate with local vocational schools and colleges to become field experiences for current students who need child care hours.

Sharon and Suzy love to cook and will be preparing take-home meals for families in need.

Lisa involved her family of college-aged children in volunteering as relief workers with local low-cost child care agencies.

Eric is partnering with his parents and their friends at the local senior residence. His young students have begun writing letters and drawing pictures as part of a Pen Pal program and Eric's Literacy for Living campaign.

outside of the box in linking families with resources and programs. She learns that not only have staff located existing resources and created partnerships, they all took ownership of this new initiative.

The director discovers that by cultivating leadership in her staff, she helped them come together to become community resources, each in his or her own unique way. Their initial efforts served as a springboard for further work in this area. They serve as an example to us all: Let us live out the message of helping our neighbor.

Lisa Ann Haeseler

Lisa Ann Haeseler is a professor of education and human services who teaches in Buffalo, New York, and Ontario, Canada. She received her doctorate from Duquesne University in interdisciplinary leadership. Lisa specializes in the area of adult domestic violence and familial abuse and is currently writing on topics such as aiding families at-risk, leadership of helping professionals, and how to further enhance educational and human service organizations.

Growing a Multi-site Organization:

Build Systems of Credibility and Empower Others to Execute Them

by Chad Dunkley

"Don't tell people how to do things. Tell them what to do and let them surprise you with their results."

George S. Patton

My mom opened a preschool classroom in a church in Brooklyn Center, Minnesota, 45 years ago. I was an enrolled student in one of our first classrooms. I became an employee about 25 years ago. Then, I became a parent and a customer of our programs. Today, I have the privilege of leading this organization as Chief Executive Officer. Over the last 45 years, I watched our organization flourish from that classroom to over 70 child care centers, caring for nearly 10,000 children per day in multiple states. In fact, we have become the largest provider in the state of Minnesota.

When you picture a large child care organization, you may see a small group of ambitious individuals sitting around a table developing plans to build an organization with a great number of locations. But the truth is, most multi-site providers grew organically because they provided outstanding child care and earned a great reputation in their community. Their programs often grew because they no longer had the capacity in one program to meet the demand for their service. This leads to the opening of another program and then as that program becomes successful, another program. That's how we ended up with some of the most significant multi-site providers in the country.

The risk of the multi-site provider, just like any other industry, is that once an organization succeeds, you must still make consistent adjustments and improvements to reflect best practices and stay on top of the current research. Just like in other fields, where you have multiple sites, you can quickly grow stale if you get complacent rather than build a culture of change in your organization. We have watched many mighty providers in the field grow and thrive, and then go through a stage where they are less successful. In fact, some multi-site providers have actually gone out of business or been acquired by organizations with more resources.

How Managing a Multi-site Organization is Different

When you direct one program, your program can be led by your individual passion for the job and your credibility. You can personally show your commitment to your families and your staff each day during frequent interactions. Many individual centers make parents feel very much a part of the center's family.

As you transition into multiple programs, it's about building systems of credibility that others can execute. It's taking management from a coach who is interacting daily with her players to someone who is a mentor and has less direct control over daily occurrences and situations. This is where delegation and empowerment come into play.

A number of years ago, because of our growth, we took on two new district managers. We selected two individuals who were terrific center directors and moved them into multi-site management positions. As they were developing in their first year and transitioning into their new roles, they had to learn how to lead in a very different way. The most important lesson they needed to learn was how to delegate responsibility to others and learn to lead by influence. They also needed to learn that each leader has a slightly different management style. Leading people who are leading others requires different skills than leading people directly. They also needed to learn to inspire and motivate at a different level. The leader needs to help people believe in the organization as a whole, not in them as individual leaders.

Early childhood programs often have the personality of the leader on-site. When you transition to a multi-site leader, you must learn where you can allow flexibility in leadership and where you must require consistency of leadership. As a multi-site manager you have to expect consistent program implementation, but you can certainly leave some flexibility for an individual teacher's creativity. As a multi-site manager, you certainly need to have fiscal policies as well as policies around health and safety that are consistently enforced. As you manage multiple site programs, you are often only as good as the reputation of your worst performing program. Word of mouth in the early childhood industry is still the most important way to either make the program successful or lead a program to failure.

One significant role for a multi-site manager or leader is to find and build systems that can produce consistent quality and customer service. Those systems need to be able to function without the daily interaction of its owner or leader. The difficult balance is finding a way to create this quality and consistency without taking away individual creativity by classroom teachers or center directors.

Best Practices in Multi-site Management

Over the years I have found that successful multi-site leaders exhibit certain strengths:

Articulating a vision. The leader must have a clear mission and vision for the organization, overall, and the ability to communicate that vision in an articulate and passionate manner. Everyone has to have the same goal in mind, no matter where individual centers are located. The organization's mission and vision need to be revisited on a consistent basis, adjusted for current market conditions and relevancy, if needed, and then communicated again to everyone on the team.

Clarifying expectations. The organization must have a clear understanding and a precise set of expectations regarding every aspect of center operation: curriculum implementation, health and safety policies and procedures, employee relations, financial accounting. There must be specific practices to monitor compliance and an established training protocol to ensure consistency.

Mastering communication. Communication is absolutely essential to the success of a multi-unit organization. Employees must know whom to contact when questions arise, and it's essential that common issues and solutions are shared across the group of centers. Successful multi-unit managers also need to know (sometimes instinctively) what must be communicated on a more global basis, and what should be handled on a more individual or regional basis.

Recruiting talent. The ability to select strong talent is very important. The multi-unit manager must know what skills, qualities, credentials, and experiences will most likely lead to success, both for the individual and the organization. With that said, it's also very important to add individuals with diverse strengths to the team.

Developing talent. The ability to develop and reward strong talent is equally important. There should be systems in place to help individuals grow in their profession, gain confidence with taking on new challenges, and understand the vital role they play in the overall success of the organization. A reward system should offer compensation and recognition, both for individual and organizational achievements.

Delegating responsibility. A multi-unit manager must be able to effectively delegate. This helps team members grow and share in the responsibility for success, and allows the multi-unit manager the ability to keep an eye on the 'big picture'; to focus on the more global issues. When I've seen multi-unit managers struggle, it's often because they feel like they must solve every problem, tackle every challenge, and manage the minute details of every project. It's simply not feasible, nor does this develop strong, confident location managers.

Building alliances. Strong multi-unit managers know how to network within the profession and build alliances that will help their organization and the entire field find success. They are members of professional organizations, stay active in trade associations, and know how to use these affiliations to look objectively at the opportunities and challenges of the organization they lead.

Developing yourself. The best multi-unit managers continue to develop themselves. They seek out opportunities for professional and personal growth, and serve as a role model for the team they lead.

Connecting staff. It's important to incorporate opportunities for staff to gather to build connections. If it's possible, gather as a group to talk about the shared mission and vision of your multi-site program. Also important is to create opportunities to do trainings together or social engagements, like going bowling for an evening, or planning a fun event together or service project.

Connecting with families. Multi-site programs should have good communication systems and family connections. Communication systems and family connections are especially valued when the organization faces what may be termed a 'significant event.' Anything newsworthy, both positive and negative or challenging, can affect not just the individual center — but the entire organization.

In early childhood, just like in any business, sometimes those who start the business as entrepreneurs are stuck in the mindset that they need to control all of the details and decisions. As a company grows, you have to trust those around you and believe they are capable of making good decisions, or even better decisions than you could in certain circumstances. As you grow in an organization, you have the ability to hire specialty expertise in areas that may not be yours. Growing to multiple sites can be an exciting, but difficult challenge; but I know from my own journey that I wouldn't have it any other way.

Chad Dunkley

Chad Dunkley is Chief Executive Officer for New Horizon Academy and Kinderberry Hill. He oversees operations, marketing, strategy, and finance, and drives the culture of 'continuous improvement' at all New Horizon and Kinderberry Hill locations. Chad received his J.D. from William Mitchell College of Law and his B.A. in management from Hamline University. Chad is President of the Minnesota Child Care Association (MCCA), on the governing board of The National Association for the Education of Young Children (NAEYC), and on the board and executive committee of The Early Care and Education Consortium.

Nine Questions for the Dedicated Board Member

by Roger Neugebauer

1. Do you understand your responsibilities as a board member?

Being a board member is not an honorary position — it entails serious obligations. The board of directors of a non profit corporation bears final responsibility for the direction and control of the organization. This involves setting goals and policies, overseeing administration, evaluating performance, and monitoring finances.

2. Is the board well organized to accomplish its responsibilities?

As volunteers, most board members can only devote a limited amount of time to board work. Therefore, it is imperative that their time be spent effectively. Most of the work of the board should take place in active committees with staff support. Meetings of committees and the full board should keep on task with the majority of time devoted to issues of the highest priority.

3. Is there an ongoing board development process?

The board should have in place an ongoing effort to recruit new board members who are committed to the goals of the organization and who bring to the board a full range of skills and perspectives. New members should have the opportunity to participate in a thorough orientation on the activities and structure of the organization and their responsibilities as board members.

4. Are board members committed to the mission of organization?

A paramount responsibility of the board is to define the short-term and long-term goals for the organization. These goals should be clearly communicated throughout the organization as well as to the community at-large. Periodically, the board should re-evaluate this mission statement in light of changing community needs and resources.

5. Does the board closely monitor the performance of the organization?

For board members to effectively carry out their responsibilities, they must keep their fingers on the pulse of the organization. They should keep in touch informally by observing the organization at work and by soliciting feedback from people the organization is serving. In addition, the board should carry out a formal periodic evaluation of the organization's progress toward achieving its goals.

6. Do board members make well-informed budgetary decisions?

The budget is an organization's most powerful policy statement. Shaping and approving the annual budget is the most important single task board members are called upon to perform. To carry out this task responsibly, they must be consulted early in the budget development process, they must be given adequate information about the financial and program implications of budget proposals, and they must deliberately weigh budget decisions in terms of the goals of the organization.

7. Does the board exercise effective oversight of the organization's financial management?

Board members should periodically review the organization's financial statements to assure that income and expenses are in line with the annual budget, and that assets and liabilities are being responsibly managed. At least annually, the board should determine whether adequate financial controls are in place. In addition, the board must approve and update a plan for the maintenance and insurance of the organization's physical assets.

8. Is there a healthy tension in relationships between board and staff members?

Unless a board abdicates its responsibility and simply acts as a rubber stamp for the staff, there are bound to be periods of tension between board and staff members. Often these tensions occur when board members overstep their bounds and inject themselves into the day-to-day operations of the organization. To prevent this, there should be a clear understanding among all parties as to the demarcation between board and staff responsibilities.

Tension can also arise when staff and board members openly disagree about a proposed course of action. While it is helpful if board and staff members can work together in harmony, board members must appreciate that their duty transcends pleasing the staff. A board member is elected by the members of the corporation to represent their interests on the board. Sometimes the interests of the members at-large do not coincide with the interests of staff members. In these cases, board members must work through these conflicts and reach decisions in the best interests of the organization. In an effectively functioning organization, such tensions are dealt with openly and professionally, with a minimum of lingering hard feelings.

9. Does the board have an effective system for evaluating the performance of the executive director?

It has been said that a strong executive director may be able to carry an organization with a weak board, but that a strong board cannot save an organization from the ill effects of a weak executive director. A board must set clear standards of performance expected of an executive director and commit itself to the ongoing task of evaluating the director's performance against those standards.

Credits

This questionnaire was developed by Exchange Press as a service to our readers. Please use it in your program. The title of this questionnaire was adapted from a form developed by Terry W. McAdam and the contents from a variety of sources including *The Nonprofit Organization Handbook* (New York: McGraw Hill Book Company, 1980) by Tracy D. Connors; A *Handbook for Day Care Board Members* (New York: Day Care Council of New York, Inc., 1984) by Christine Dimock Secor; *The Board of Directors of Nonprofit Organizations* (Washington, DC: Management Assistance Group, 1977) by Karl Mathiasen, III; and *Evaluating the Performance of Trustees and School Heads* (Boston: National Association of Independent Schools, 1986) by Eric W. Johnson.

Roger Neugebauer

Roger Neugebauer is publisher of *Exchange Magazine* and a co-founder of the World Forum Foundation.

Enjoying the Good Lice

Managing Crises

by Pauline Davey Zeece

"It is what we do rather than what we feel or say we do that reflects who and what we truly are."

Leo Buscaglia quoted by D. Lynch and P. Kordis in *Strategy of the Dolphin: Scoring a Win in a Chaotic World* (Ballentine Books, 1988)

The first time I ever saw lice hopping from curl to curl on a small child's head was over 15 years ago. The critters were so small and quick (the lice that is) that I had to blink twice before I could process what I was seeing. And when the realization finally struck me, I felt compelled to shift my weight, to scratch my scalp… and, quite honestly, to exit quickly.

To make matters worse, one of the other teachers who had also never seen lice but who believed that "such things only inflicted impoverished people" had systematically checked the heads of 22 children with the same comb. By the end of the week, the school was involved in a lice crisis of major proportions. Teachers, staff, children, and families had been afflicted and the local pharmacist had become wealthy.

I am pleased to report that the outbreak claimed no long-term casualties; everyone did survive. In subsequent times and other places amidst a lice event, I have been more able to act effectively. I now am actually beginning to control my head scratching. You might say that I am learning from lice, or at least from their presence in early childhood programs.

With this in mind, how can administrators learn to manage this and other crises constructively and to use these as opportunities for learning?

"The sky is falling, the sky is falling."

Chicken Little

Best Kept Crisis Secrets

• Crises happen.

Crises are a predictable part of life, and therefore a predictable part of child care programming. Quality programming is not necessarily characterized by absence of crisis; instead, it is identified by presence of effective crisis management. Accepting that crises will and do occur is the first step in dealing with them well.

Another important part of crisis management is understanding how crises happens — this can be accomplished by actually charting crisis events. In doing this, a director can develop a crisis pattern or profile for a program. Such a profile typically consists of five W's: what, when, where, who, and why.

What. Understanding the 'what' of a crisis can be deceptively simple. This is particularly true when crisis is interpersonal rather than programmatic in nature. A cook who walks off the job 30 minutes before lunch or a child with a broken finger is a clearly recognizable crisis. But a group of parents who collectively decide not to support a teacher or a staff person who burns out is less specifically pinpointed.

Really understanding what happens in a crisis entails separating facts from interpretation. For example, "The cook left the building at 11:30 am today and said she was never coming back" is a fact. "The cook stomped out of the kitchen and quit because she was angry at everyone" is an interpretation. Both bits of information are useful, but in different ways. Collecting facts over time about programmatic crises enables a director to chart events and sometimes to predict and head off disaster before it strikes.

Interpersonal crises may be less easily charted. These may need to be monitored by attending closely to the interpretation of a fact or a collection of facts surrounding a crisis. For example, the fact that "Marba hasn't smiled or spoken to anyone in the center for a week" may be less critical information in dealing with an interpersonal crisis than the interpretation that "Marba is burning out and has appeared depressed and withdrawn for some time." Most times, crises are handled best when accurate facts and interpretation are considered.

When. It should not come as a surprise to learn that more accidents involving young children occur when adults and/or children are tired, hungry, bored, or under undue stress. When you think about it, this includes just about everything that happens to adults and children in a child care setting but sleep. And anyone who has spent time in a nap room can testify that this, too, can be a hazard area.

Crises then are affected by timing. Right before lunch and nap and late afternoon are prime times for children to get hurt. And hurt children precipitate crises of all sorts. Charting when crises occur in a program can help a director identify critical periods.

Adults can also have identifiable 'down times' in child care settings. It would be helpful to learn what contributes to these times in your program. Take a few minutes to jot down the last five crises with which you have dealt. When did these occur? Do you see a pattern? Were these adult or child crises (or both)? What can you learn from understanding the timing of these events?

Where. As children and adults learn to live and work with each other in a child care setting, they construct cognitive maps about how the space around them is to be used. What this means for young children is that they develop ideas about where things should happen — this is where I play blocks, this is where I sleep when it is naptime, this is where I run. Crisis looms when there are unclear messages about space usage or when people live and work together for long hours each day in an overcrowded child care setting. Without clear boundaries, both children and adults are more apt to experience difficulties.

In the lab school, we have a wonderful patch of mature pine trees that children call the 'forest.' When weather permits, teachers will often take tents and camp in this forest with children. A minor crisis evolved with the grounds department when the shrubbery around the camping area began to die... it appears some children were taking a rustic approach to toileting. Obviously, the cognitive map for camping at school and at home had not been clearly drawn.

On a more serious note, 'where' may also contribute to interpersonal crises. Where do you speak with staff or parents when there is a problem? Is it always in the same place? What else happens there? Do you ask staff to trust and share openly in this same place? Is it on your turf or theirs? Or, better still, is it ever in a neutral location?

"No one is ever old enough to know better."

Holbrook Jackson quoted by Jon Winokur in *Friendly Advice* (Dutton, 1990)

The last two W's (who and why) fall under the next secret about crises.

• Blame doesn't work.

Who. Blame for the sake of blame builds neither individual character nor strong early childhood programs. Equally important, it has never been demonstrated that self-flogging clears the mind or sharpens the skills of a child care administrator. Thus, the importance of understanding 'who' rests in the power of unraveling the roles everyone plays during a crisis.

The work of child care is a collaborative effort; nothing happens in a vacuum. The good and bad, out. But equally useful to understand would be how every person, as well as the demands of the cook's job itself, contributed to an unmanageable situation for one person.

Charting the 'who' of crises in a program allows an administrator to see a different kind of worker profile. Over time it can be determined if one or two workers are always in the eye of the storm or if others are always the ones to calm the waters and pick up the pieces. Both groups of people need support in different ways.

As your profile begins to develop, look to see where you fit. What role do you typically play during crisis? How would workers categorize you if they were developing their own profile?

Why. Asking 'why' in the heat of a crisis is like demanding that a three year old explain why she stuck a grape up her nose. In both instances, 'why' usually does little to solve the immediate situation or to shed light on a long-term solution. Thus, 'why' is best asked after the passion of the moment has subsided and after all the other W's have been processed.

This is so because 'why' is the interaction among the 'who,' 'when,' 'where,' and 'what' of a crisis.

When management of crisis is approached in this way, the 'why' of a difficult situation may actually be understood before anyone even poses the question. Understanding the 'why' of a crisis also allows directors to polish their own panic and increase their own effectiveness in dealing with crisis. This occurs when directors:

■ take time to understand the role model they set within a program and to learn how their response matches those of others.

■ set time for regular 'crisis drills' to discuss the merits of solving hypothetical crises in a variety of ways.

■ recognize and reward effective crisis resolution in an ongoing way within their programs.

"It often happens that we only become aware of the importance of facts if we suppress the question 'Why?' and then in the course of our investigation these facts lead us to an answer."

Ludwig Wittgenstein quoted by D. Lynch and P. Kordis in *Strategy of the Dolphin: Scoring a Win in a Chaotic World* (Ballentine Books, 1988)

But this is not to say that every crisis can be accurately anticipated, perfectly dissected, or even clearly understood. There are things that happen in day-to-day life that cannot always be explained; there are also circumstances over which an administrator may have little or no control. Thus, like all of the other W's, why is only one of many tools to be used to better manage crisis.

• Not all crises are bad.

The last best kept secret is that crises is not always bad. Granted, when children or adults get hurt, when people lose self-respect or self-esteem, when resources or circumstances dictate impossible decisions where no one feels good about the outcome, crises injures a program. But in other instances, it may actually be instructive or even healthy.

Through effective crisis management, one can come to the understanding that all crises are potential opportunities for learning. As such, directors learn to assign and/or accept responsibility for error without condemning themselves or others and without giving up. They learn to put each crisis on a continuum and to ask themselves: "What is the importance and the consequence of this action today, tomorrow, next month, next year?"

And, finally, directors can learn to evaluate the full spectrum of crisis effects. When crisis damages beyond repair, it brings a special kind of challenge to an administrator. When crisis discourages, it is, at best, cumbersome. When crisis devastates people or programs, it is destructive.

"The play-it-all pessimists of the world never accomplish much of anything because they don't look clearly and objectively at situations, they don't recognize or believe in their own abilities,and they won't stretch their abilities to overcome even the smallest amount of risk."

Benjamin Hoff in *The Tao of Pooh*
(Penguin Books, 1982)

But when crisis fosters close inspection of philosophy, policy, or practice, it is useful. When crisis requires collective ownership of a mutual problem and mandates collaborative solution, it is powerful. When crisis butts heads with apathy and paves the way for meaningful and effective change, it is worth the effort it engenders.

Crises can be crippling if they are not taken seriously. But competent administrators learn to monitor the pulse of a program so as to best understand the magnitude of a crisis and its fall out.

Effective managers then are able to use crises to learn and to make their programs better and stronger and less vulnerable the next time around.

References

Hoff, B. (1982). *The tao of Pooh.* New York: Penguin Books.

Jackson, H. (1990). *Friendly advice.* New York: Dutton.

Lynch, D., & Kordis, P. (1988). *Strategy of the dolphin: Scoring a win in a chaotic world.* New York: Ballentine Books.

Pauline Davey Zeece

Pauline Davey Zeece is currently an Emeritus Professor at the University of Nebraska-Lincoln. Although she has been retired from UNL for several years, she still remains active in consulting with several major textbook publishers in the development of a variety of educational supplements.

Considering Expansion?

Lessons Learned Along the Way

by Henry Wilde

I recently flashed back to a conversation I had almost 15 years ago — soon after we started Acelero Learning — with a manager at a Head Start program we were working with at the time. We were coaching this organization to use data effectively, and we had driven their move from paper-based management to an electronic child data management system (which, though hard to believe now, was a challenge). The manager was trying to capture child screening results in the data system and innocently asked how I would define the terms in a specific data field: Does 'complete' mean the same as 'pass'? Was a developmental screening still 'complete'"if the child refused to participate, or should that be counted as 'failed'? I remember thinking how trivial these questions were. I told her, "As long as you are consistent, just do whatever makes sense to you."

Flash forward. Today, our organization operates in 40 buildings in four different states with hundreds of employees capturing child data. In a review of child health outcomes, we found disparities across regions that we could not explain. When we burrowed deep into the data, do you know what we found? Our results were different, because in the very same fields I had discussed with that manager a dozen years earlier, our staff had defined the data the way that made the most sense to them — which varied at every site! Over the course of the last year, we have developed

our own proprietary data system, Shine Insight, and I have been struck by the number of hours we have dedicated to a larger version of this very same question. Whenever I feel like we are spending too much time wrestling with a tedious detail, I remind myself of the lightbulb that has illuminated our work so many times before: Building and managing an individual program effectively is not the same challenge as replicating success at scale.

Our mission is to bring a relentless focus on positive child and family outcomes to close the achievement gap to build a better future for the children, families, and communities served by the Head Start program. When we began our work in 2001, we had two employees, and had never run a Head Start program before. Nearly 15 years later, we have 1,000 employees and serve nearly 5,000 children and through Shine Early Learning, our sister organization, we impact over 30,000 children in Head Start programs that are focused on adapting our tools and approaches for use in their contexts.

But growth is really hard. We still struggle with the explicit choices and question the implicit choices we have made about how and when to grow and how to maintain quality at scale. If we serve more children but our child outcomes stagnate or decline, we have abdicated our mission. On the flip side, growing the organization can provide additional resources, which ultimately unlock greater quality and better child and family outcomes. We think we have been successful at striking the balance, but some days more than others. (Right now, for instance, we have decided not to pursue growth opportunities for the foreseeable future and to focus on innovation and strengthening our current operations.) I wish that the five major lessons we have learned could provide you with answers, but I fear that is unlikely. Instead, I hope they prompt questions you might ask yourselves if you are considering expansion.

Lesson 1:
Determine what is core to your model before you grow.

In our early days as an organization, we believed that if we disseminated the same curriculum, policies, and procedures, used the same data systems, and held our programs to the same quantitative outcome measures — and did it better than everyone else did — that we would get better results for kids. We gave our regional directors almost unbound latitude around execution, because our assumption was that local managers would use that flexibility to solve problems in innovative ways better than we could from a central office. While we were partially correct, we fell short in four important ways.

First, our programs followed a herd of other early childhood education programs without questioning why. We built a model premised on the belief that we would do the same things as every other program we knew, only better, but we never questioned the sacred cows. Do we know of programs that are demonstrating breakthrough outcomes? And if not, should the core of our model be trying to use the same curriculum and assessments and performance standards as everyone else? Or should the core of our model be something entirely different?

Second, when we brought world-class content area experts into our central office, they often disagreed with the leadership at the local level about who had decision-making rights. We told our regional

executive directors that they were responsible for everything that happened in their programs; but the national experts in our central office tried to adapt the fundamental elements of our program approach and were not informed about local deviations. We lost quality control. As one of our regional Executive Directors told me, "There is a lot of room to undermine and deprioritize at the local level if we disagree."

Third, the experts who ultimately developed and disseminated the content that became the Acelero model did not know how to effectively support execution, because each center director made dozens of incrementally different decisions (tweaked a form, altered a procedure, modified a training, skipped a curriculum unit) from her colleagues down the road and thousands of miles away.

Fourth, we lost the benefit of our network. We believed that learning what worked across the network would lead to replicable breakthrough solutions, but it was not an expectation layered into how we collectively improved. Instead, we had brilliant people doing amazing work all over the country, but we were not codifying or replicating their work everywhere.

Listed are some changes we made along the way, and where we stand today:

■ We purposefully question why we do what we do. It was a difficult but game changing epiphany when we realized that what we thought of as the fundamental pieces of our operating model were, in fact, a trope. The core of how our programs operate today only emerged when we forced ourselves to question whether we have evidence that the choices we make actually result in better outcomes for children and families. Listed are some of those choices:

• Our curriculum and assessment systems are far more scaffolded than they were, and as a result, variations in execution are within a narrower band, and our support and monitoring of implementation is more robust.

- We no longer allow Center Directors to come from general management or family services roles, as they once did; Center Directors must be educators first and foremost.

- Our approach to parent engagement and family goal setting is no longer intended to be all things to all people. We have integrated into every interaction we have with families — from the first day they enroll — the explicit understanding that parents are expected to partner with us to ensure that their children are on par with their middle-income peers when they get to kindergarten. We create settings where parents can develop social capitol with one another. But we no longer force every family to walk through the same regimented goal-setting process, regardless of their needs. We purposefully differentiate services for families in crisis from families with significant health needs or those who express the desire to set self-sufficiency goals and provide better support as a result.

- ■ Our local Executive Directors still have wide decision-making latitude, but within the confines of the core elements of our programmatic model. We invested countless hours of senior leadership time to work through and clarify decision rights between local leadership and central leadership, which resulted in a detailed matrix I still keep handy today.

- ■ We have a process for piloting new programmatic initiatives, we codify innovations better, and our cycle for launching new innovations is consistent year-over-year and explicitly incorporates the insights of our brightest and most talented leaders across the network.

- ■ We now hold at least three summits per year for leaders across our network in each service area to ensure that we are learning from one another. When we are considering network-wide improvements or deciding upon whether to expand a pilot, our most talented senior leaders from across the network have input — but there is also clear understanding that ultimately, the content area

leader at the central office has final decision-making rights on our programmatic model.

In short, we have tried to distill what makes our model successful and done everything we can to put in place structures to maximize the likelihood that we can replicate — while continuing to evolve — those core elements in every one of our programs.

Lesson 2:
Solve problems as you go, but take notes.

When we started, we envisioned reaching 10,000 children every year in life-changing Head Start programs. We did not know how we would do it, but our deepest-held belief was that we would solve any problem that could deter us from meeting our mission; and we still feel that way. With that said, our greatest strength — our determination to solve problems as they arose — proved to be a double-edged sword when we faced a similar problem the second and third time around. What were the nine steps we took to fix that issue last time? Did we even write down what we did? And could we explain and train somebody else to do the same?

As we course corrected, we often referenced the distinction (described first for us in *Built to Last*, Collins & Porras, 2004) between time tellers and clock builders. As the authors explained:

"Having a great idea or being a charismatic visionary leader is 'time telling'; building a company that can prosper far beyond the tenure of any single leader and through multiple product lifecycles is 'clock building.'"

We did not want to become individual performers who could not replicate our results. We could continue to address issues as they came up, but we had to think more proactively about how someone else would do it the next time. We needed to transition from a small group of entrepreneurial generalists to a team of skilled people with well-defined and more specialized job responsibilities. If you do not consider the future when you grow your organization, you will take two steps backwards before you move forward.

Lesson 3:
Do not confuse exemplars with consistent execution.

We begin each leadership meeting with a ritual borrowed from City Year in which we share "Ripples of Hope" from across our network. Drawn from a Bobby Kennedy speech delivered in apartheid South Africa, each ripple of hope represents a small event involving a child or family in one of our centers, which both reminds us of why we do the work we do and reflects the impact our work can have when done well. These ripples inspire and sustain all of us. But as we grow, we must always remember that our goal is — as Kennedy says later in the quote — for individual ripples to build a "mighty current which can sweep down the mightiest walls of oppression and resistance."

Growing your organization into a mighty current can be trying and exhausting work, and our natural tendency is to cling to the stories that bring our work to life: the child whose mother visits your center to share that her child is ahead of his peers in kindergarten; the father who was inspired to return to school to become a preschool teacher by volunteering in his daughter's class; the child who had been expelled from multiple centers before coming to yours and has now met the goals of his IEP; and so many more. But when you grow, you must be careful not to allow individual ripples to obscure ineffectiveness or inconsistency of quality. Every child and family we serve should be part of the current.

Lesson 4:
Know your path to financial sustainability, and grow in manageable steps.

Child care is a brutal business; practitioners enter the field because they care about children, not to become titans of industry; and the varying landscapes of child care subsidy, Head Start, and state and local pre-K add complexity, particularly for providers like us whose mission is specifically to serve low-income families. These complications are very real and cause child care providers to hunker down to try to protect the business they have or to grow when opportunity arises without a clear plan. As a result, some wonderful providers do not adapt and ultimately succumb to competition or financial pressures, and others grow too fast and unsustainably.

There are no magic elixirs for adapting to changing markets. We have experienced this ourselves in multiple locations when public policy decisions and unforeseen market forces have slowed us on our anticipated path to full enrollment and financial stability. But complexity and unplanned developments or undesirable public policy decisions are not reasons for failing to plan. You need to anticipate likely financial scenarios, identify contingencies, and when circumstances change, revisit your plan. Investing ahead of the curve is preferable, but without favorable financing, an endowment, independent wealth, or large retained earnings, you must carefully consider how to make incremental investments to match the ramp-up of payments coming through the door. We cannot dismiss the financial side of growing to scale as the unsavory underbelly of an otherwise noble profession. It is crucial to achieving our mission.

Lesson 5:
Nothing is more crucial than identifying and training leaders who share your organization's values, have the right skills, and can grow with the company.

When we expand into new markets, we do more than put up new signs and change the names on the licenses. We are building a new corporate culture, imparting a new mission, new values, and a new language, and implementing new systems and curriculum. When we grow, we create opportunities for talented employees who might not otherwise have seen a path to grow professionally in our organization to take on greater responsibilities in new programs. These rising leaders help introduce their new colleagues to our operational policies and procedures, but more importantly, they imprint the organization's DNA into new programs. Every hire and managerial decision they make reflects their experience and the standards of quality, the mission, and the values of our organization. If your organization has cultivated a pipeline of future leaders, this cycle can be virtuous: you retain your best talent by creating meaningful professional development tracks. If, however, your talent pipeline is bare, or the drain of talent required to satisfy your plans for growth impedes the success of existing centers, trying to scale up may be harmful to achieving your mission.

If you are like us, you spend most of your revenue on salaries and benefits. Your people are your product. If you look around at your current staff and cannot imagine anyone at the table capable of leading a new program, you need to reevaluate who you are hiring and retaining and how you are supporting employees who aspire to grow. We have found that many of our most effective employees have no interest in moving on or assuming additional responsibilities, and we hope they will stay with us forever. But we have also begun to systematically invest in our highest performing leaders who express an interest in growing with us — by creating Director-in-Waiting tracks for teachers and a Leadership Cohort of hand-selected managers, which we hope will prepare us for future growth.

In Conclusion

We feel a tremendous sense of urgency about our work. We serve children for two years, and our mission is to close the achievement gap before they leave the program. Growth is hard, and we make mistakes, but the children we are serving cannot wait for us to figure everything out each time we open a new center or move into a new region. A few years ago, we hosted Bonnie St. John, an awe-inspiring Para-Olympic skiing silver medalist — and a Head Start graduate — who shared a key lesson from her skiing career: "I learned that people fall down, winners get up, and gold medal winners just get up faster."

At Acelero, we anticipated some of the challenges I have described, but others we learned (and continue to learn) by falling. I hope that our experiences can benefit other organizations considering the same path. One thing I know for sure: If your organization is going to grow to scale — to enter new markets, open more centers, and serve more children — the most important thing is to learn from your mistakes and get up faster next time than you did the last.

Reference

Collins, J., & Porras, J. I. (2004). *Built to last: Successful habits of visionary companies.* New York: HarperBusiness.

Henry Wilde

Henry Wilde is the Co-Founder of Acelero Learning, a company explicitly dedicated to closing the achievement gap for young children served in the Head Start program. Founded in 2001, Acelero provides high-quality early childhood education to nearly 5,000 children from low-income families and offers training and technical assistance to Head Start programs around the country. Wilde previously served as the Deputy Secretary for the Department of Children and Families for the State of Wisconsin, where he coordinated the launch of YoungStar, Wisconsin's child care Quality Rating and Improvement System. He began his career working as a Special Assistant to Marian Wright Edelman at the Children's Defense Fund, after graduating from Harvard University. He is an Ascend Fellow and a Pahara Fellow at the Aspen Institute.

Out of the Box Ideas for Center Evaluation

by Roger Neugebauer

The challenges of managing an early childhood program are myriad. As a director, you can easily get so caught up in dealing with daily crises that you never have time to step back and evaluate how the center is doing. So I have compiled a list of indicators, which, while not exactly scientific in their precision, are nonetheless in my experience reliable ways to judge whether your program is headed in the right or wrong direction, quality-wise.

Turnover Rates

Most recent research has pointed accusing fingers at turnover as a major deterrent to center quality. Frequent turnover causes anxiety among children and parents. It also undermines team building and program development efforts. If you are spending significant time every month finding replacements for teachers, this is a real problem.

Clearly, centers that pay significantly higher salaries have lower turnover rates. However, in my experience, centers operating under the same financial and environmental constraints can have dramatically different turnover rates. In centers where the director is a good leader, where staff morale is high, teachers want to stay.

However, while all would agree that high turnover undermines quality, it may also be true that near-zero turnover is not the ultimate goal. Teacher longevity is not always an indicator of teacher performance. While some teachers may improve on the job every day for 20 years, others may become set in their ways or less inspired in what they do. An effective director is equally conscientious in supporting and supervising the work of experienced and inexperienced teachers.

Absentee Rates

In centers where staff morale is low, staff not only leave more often, but they also find more ways to be away from the center. Staff absenteeism typically rises and falls in inverse relationship to staff morale. Since center leave policies and scheduling practices are so varied, there is no single measure of absenteeism that will work for all centers. What needs to be measured is the frequency with which staff take unplanned or unexpected leave.

One useful indicator is sick leave. If teachers use 100% of their sick leave allotment in a year, this is a strong indicator of organizational malaise. In centers with highly committed staff, directors often need to convince dedicated teachers to take sick leave when they are ill.

A second indicator would be unscheduled absences or tardiness. It is understandable that sometimes teachers may experience personal crises at home that prevents them from showing up on time or sometimes from showing up at all. A center needs to have a back-up plan for dealing with such occasions. But if unscheduled absences are becoming commonplace, this is a strong indicator that staff are losing their commitment to the program.

Occupancy Rates

Since centers operate so close to the margin, a small difference in an occupancy rate can make a big difference in resources available to enhance quality. Moving a center from an 85% to a 90% occupancy rate can have a huge impact on the availability of curriculum resources, the amount of staff training, and the staffing ratios at the beginning and end of the day.

To a large extent, occupancy rates are affected by factors outside of the control of directors. The state of the local economy, the supply of child care in the community, the rates charged by other centers, and trends in the population of young children all impact occupancy. However, operating within these constraints, an effective director can do much to improve occupancy. To begin with, the effective director keeps in touch with changing consumer needs. In addition, she knows how to recruit new parents and how to retain them once they commit. Effective directors may also be skillful in negotiating service contracts with local employers or public agencies.

There are two ways to evaluate occupancy rates. First, compare the occupancy rate of your center with other centers in the community. If your occupancy is higher than most centers in the community, this is good news — you must be doing something right. If your rate is lower than everyone else, this is bad news — you must be doing something wrong.

On the other hand, if your occupancy is declining, but other centers in your community are experiencing a similar challenge, it probably means your program is being impacted by changes in the local economy beyond your immediate control.

A second way to evaluate occupancy is to measure your center's occupancy month by month. Watch for trends. If your occupancy is steadily declining over a period of months, you need to take action immediately to reverse this trend. Conducting exit interviews with parents who disenroll is crucial. You need to find out the cause for the decline: is a new center offering better rates or more flexible hours?; are parents upset because a favorite teacher has left?; are parents having a hard time convincing children to stay at the center? Finding out the cause early, and taking action to fix it, can help maintain a healthy occupancy level.

Return Rates

Financiers measure the success of their investments by their return rates — the percent of profit an investment returns. Centers can measure their success by another form of return rate — the rate at which families return to the center.

For centers that have been in business for less than 10 years, there is only one return rate that applies — the frequency with which families return to the center to enroll their subsequent children. If families routinely enroll additional children in a center, this is a probable sign that the center is doing something right. I emphasize the qualifier *probable* because for parents, the convenience of having children in one location may weigh heavily in enrollment decisions.

For centers that have been serving families for more than 10 years, a second return rate comes into play — people who graduated from a center returning to work as teachers. If a teenager who spent a significant portion of his early years at your center applies for a job, this is a strong indication that your center provided a positive experience for that child. No qualifiers here — this is 100% good news.

Finally, for centers that have been around for more than 20 years, there is a third return rate — people who graduated from a center returning to enroll their own children. Once again, this return rate is a solid indicator that the children in your center are having a memorable and positive experience. What more perfect testimonial could there be than to have attendees of your program wanting to share this experience with their own children?

Discipline Problems

At early childhood conferences, workshops on discipline or classroom management are always packed. This gives the impression that discipline problems are inevitable in centers. However, when I visit well-managed centers with effective teachers, discipline is a non-issue. Good teachers know how to structure the environment and present activity choices so that children are continuously engaged.

The amount of time devoted to managing the challenging behaviors of children is a reliable indicator of the experiences children are having in your classrooms. If discipline continues to be a nagging issue, this likely indicates that children are bored and uninvolved and are venting their frustrations through anti-social behavior.

Screen Time

Study after study has been released in recent years showing that preschool children today are spending more and more time in front of screens — television screens, computer screens, and cell phone screens. In general, the conclusion is that spending so much time in front of screens is an impediment to normal physical, emotional, social, and cognitive development.

That is not to say that all screen time is bad time. As technology advances, there certainly will be more and more programs that support the appropriate social and cognitive development of young children. And, when young children are able to talk and view their grandparents who live far away or their parents who may be traveling on business via interactive programs, this certainly is healthy and important.

But children need to spend significant amounts of time in active play, in exploring the real world and not just the virtual world, in being outdoors learning to appreciate and connect with the natural world. Monitoring and controlling the amount of time children in your center are engaged in screen time makes a big difference — particularly in a time when society in general is pushing in the opposite direction.

Child Views

In the business world, companies typically assess their performance by checking the opinions of their customers. Likewise, child care centers frequently survey parents as one means of gauging their performance. This feedback is always useful. If a large number of parents have concerns about your program, you absolutely need to know about this so you can take action.

A seldom explored additional consumer evaluation is to survey children in the center. They often spend more time in your center than you do, so certainly their attitudes about the place should carry some weight. Of course, surveying children as consumers of your services requires some creative questioning. Asking four year olds to rate the quality of your center on a scale of 1 to 10 would not yield particularly helpful results. On the other hand, it may be useful to ask them what they most like to do at the center, what they like most about their teachers, and what they don't like doing. Such questions have the potential of yielding patterns of responses that are instructive about children's experiences.

Affection

In our increasingly litigious society, it is not surprising that teachers are becoming reluctant to display outward signs of affection to children for fear of being accused of child abuse.

This, of course, is terribly wrong. Centers need to head off accusations of abuse by working hard to develop trusting relationships with parents, to encourage them to share even the smallest concerns before they mushroom into big concerns, to assure them that staff are carefully selected and well supervised, and to invite them to visit unannounced at any time.

The worst possible response is to withhold affection from children. The relationship between children and teachers is a critical factor in the children's ability to develop trust, to develop friendships, to experience the joys of human interactions. Children need affection as part of their daily lives.

From time to time, it is instructive to take an affection audit at your center. Walk around casually and observe how often you see teachers showing affection to children either by physical contact, body language, or direct communication. If you see a great deal of appropriate affection being exhibited, take this as a good sign; if there is very little taking place, you need to figure out why and do something about it.

Laughter

Child care centers should be joyful places for children and adults. When I visit a center where everyone is quiet, reserved, or — even worse — somber, red flags go up. I dislike spending long periods of time with people who are unhappy, and I can't imagine spending day after day, week after week in such a somber environment.

While you are walking about the center doing an affection audit, keep your ears open for laughter, too. Children and staff do not need to be laughing all the time, of course. There are many occasions where people in the center will be appropriately involved without laughter, such as when a child is deeply engaged in an activity or when a teacher is talking to a child about something that is troubling her. On balance, however, every hour in every classroom should yield a great deal of happiness.

As noted at the outset, these are not scientifically researched measures of center quality. But without engaging in a full-scale, expensive center evaluation, these indicators can give you an informal means of identifying potential signs of trouble and assessing whether your program is headed in the right direction.

Roger Neugebauer

Roger Neugebauer is publisher of *Exchange Magazine* and a co-founder of the World Forum Foundation.

Do You Have a Healthy Organization?

by Roger Neugebauer

For a body to be healthy, a myriad of bodily functions must operate in perfect harmony. Likewise, for an organization to be healthy, a complex array of interpersonal and administrative functions must be addressed simultaneously. A serious deficiency in any one function can throw the others out of balance and undermine the organization's overall ability to perform.

Organizational psychologists have begun developing instruments for giving organizational check-ups. Their diagnoses pinpoint areas of stress and malfunctioning. *Exchange* has analyzed several dozen of these instruments in terms of their applicability to the child care setting.

The following "Organizational Health Checklist" incorporates 40 criteria for an effective child care organization selected from these instruments. This battery is by no means complete — some instruments include several thousand factors to be assessed — but, in the author's opinion, it includes the major factors an administrator in this labor-intensive, resource-poor field should be concerned with.

In rating your organization against these criteria, several cautions should be kept in mind. First, the criteria as stated represent the optimum level of functioning for a healthy organization. It is unlikely that any organization could perfectly satisfy every criteria at one time. The criteria should be viewed as goals to strive toward, not as minimal standards. The purposes of the criteria are to help you identify your organization's strengths and weaknesses and to enable you to develop strategies for improving the performance of your organization.

Second, you should keep in mind that as administrator of your organization your perspective on these criteria will be far from objective. So, in addition to rating the center yourself, you should seek to have members from different vantage points within the organization, as well as knowledgeable outside parties, perform the rating. By comparing ratings from these various perspectives, you will probably get a more accurate reading on your organization's health.

Early Childhood Organizational Health Checklist

Planning and Evaluation

1. The organization has defined its mission and has developed a manageable list of specific goals for the curriculum and for the organization as a whole.

2. Members of the organization helped shape these goals, are well aware of them, and are motivated to achieve them.

3. Strategies for accomplishing these goals have been implemented. The organization pays more than lip service to the goals. Its daily activities are directed toward achieving them.

4. The organization has developed an ongoing process for evaluating progress toward achieving the goals.

5. The evaluation process is taken seriously at all levels in the organization. Staff members are continuously searching for ways to improve the organization's performance.

6. Evaluation findings are acted upon. Strengths identified are supported and weaknesses are remedied. The organization does not shy away from abandoning or reworking low performing activities and unachievable goals.

Motivation and Control

7. All staff members take the quality of the organization's services seriously.

8. All staff members know their roles in the organization, as well as the specific tasks they are to perform.

9. Staff members exercise self-control over their own performance. They are motivated to perform well out of their commitment to achieving the organization's goals, not out of fear of punishment or desire for financial rewards.

10. Staff burnout is minimized by giving staff members considerable responsibility for managing their own work, by providing variety in their work assignments and training opportunities, and by offering whatever support they need to perform well.

11. Staff members accept the value of constructive conformity to necessary organizational rules and procedures.

12. Staff members perceive salaries and fringe benefits as being administered equitably and fairly.

Group Functioning

13. Staff members feel they are a part of a group and have a sense of loyalty to the organization.

14. Staff members freely cooperate. They share resources, ideas, and experiences.

15. Staff members feel comfortable enough in the group to openly express their feelings. The exchange of negative, as well as positive, feedback is accepted and encouraged.

16. Conflict over ideas — goals, philosophies, methods, or results — is fostered by the organization.

17. Conflict over personal issues is dealt with directly through confrontation or negotiation, rather than by smoothing it over or ignoring it.

18. Communication flows freely and accurately in all directions. Plans, problems, decisions, and developments are shared freely by the director; and problems, suggestions, and criticisms are routinely brought to the director's attention by subordinates.

Staff Development

19. The organization assigns high priority to the staff recruitment and selection process so as to assure that the staff has sufficient skills to accomplish the organization's goals.

20. The organization's leadership has complete confidence in the skills of staff members and makes every effort to tap these skills to the fullest extent.

21. Staff members, in conversation with the organizations leaders, set their own training objectives and strategies and assume responsibility for carrying them out. The organization's leadership supports their efforts by providing, whenever possible, the resources they require for self-development.

22. Staff members assume responsibility for supporting each other in their efforts to develop to their full potential.

23. Staff members continually provide each other with objective feedback on the effects of their performance and behavior. Performance appraisal is a daily, not yearly, occurrence.

24. Staff creativity is encouraged by providing an idea-rich environment and by fostering a permissive atmosphere for brainstorming and experimentation.

Decision Making and Problem Solving

25. Problems are identified and addressed early — before they get out of hand.

26. Staff members most directly affected by, or involved with, a decision either has responsibility for making the decision on their own or has major input before a decision is made.

27. Parents' feedback on their experiences and those of their children are regularly solicited and consistently responded to.

28. Decisions, once made, are communicated to all affected members of the organization and are implemented in full.

Financial Management

29. The organization develops a formal annual budget. The budget is viewed as a means of accomplishing the organization's goals for the year. It is based on a realistic projection of the expenditures required to achieve the goals and the revenues likely to be generated.

30. The organization has a sound accounting system that incorporates adequate safeguards against mismanagement and theft and that generates required reports on a timely basis.

31. Monthly financial status reports are utilized to monitor the actual implementation of the budget.

32. Cash flow is projected at least 12 months in advance.

33. The organization carries out a routine schedule for property and equipment inspection and maintenance.

Environmental Interaction

34. The organization is effective in collecting information on new ideas and new resources, as well as in processing this information for use in developing the organization.

35. The organization has an ongoing plan for marketing its services throughout the community.

36. The organization takes full and appropriate advantage of the latest social media tools in communicating with parents and promoting the program.

37. Members of the organization actively participate in efforts to influence public policy decisions, which impact on the organization.

38. The organization is effective in securing adequate financial and in-kind resources from public and/or private sources.

39. The organization maintains its autonomy by drawing resources from a wide range of external sources, thus not becoming overly dependent on any one source.

40. The organization is alert to changes in consumer needs, political moods, and economic conditions so that strategies can be developed in time for reacting to these changes.

Roger Neugebauer

Roger Neugebauer is publisher of *Exchange Magazine* and a co-founder of the World Forum Foundation.